AmblesideOnline Poetry Anthology Volume Two

Walter de la Mare
Eugene Field
James Whitcomb Riley
Christina Rossetti

Edited and annotated
by the
AmblesideOnline
Educational Foundation

AmblesideOnline Poetry Anthology Volume Two: Walter de la Mare, Eugene Field, James Whitcomb Riley, Christina Rossetti

Copyright © 2021 by AmblesideOnline Educational Foundation

Cover design by Bryan White

All rights reserved. No part of this publication may be reproduced, stored in a retrieval system or transmitted in any form by any means, electronic, mechanical, photocopy, recording or otherwise, without the prior permission of the publisher, except as provided by U.S. copyright law.

ISBN: 9798453215225

Table of Contents

Introduction to the Series i

Foreword to Volume Two iii

Walter de la Mare (1873-1956) 1

    "Between Waking and Dreaming": Biographical Sketch by Anne White 1

    01. The Horseman 3

    02. Up and Down 3

    03. Mrs. Earth 3

    04. Tired Tim 4

    05. I Can't Abear 4

    06. Some One 4

    07. The Little Bird 5

    08. The Cupboard 5

    09. Hide and Seek 6

    10. The Window 7

    11. A Widow's Weeds 7

    12. The Little Green Orchard 8

    13. King David 9

    14. The Old House 10

    15. Unstooping 10

    16. All but Blind 11

    17. Nicholas Nye 11

18. Five Eyes..13

19. Summer Evening..13

20. Earth Folk 13

21. The Ruin 14

22. Trees...14

23. Silver 15

24. Nobody Knows 16

25. Wanderers 17

26. Many a Mickle 17

27. Will Ever? 18

28. The Song of the Secret 19

29. The Song of the Soldiers 19

30. The Bees' Song... 20

31. Song of Enchantment... 21

32. Dream Song.. 21

34. The Song of the Mad Prince..23

35. The Song of Finis 23

36. November (also called Autumn) 24

37. The Scribe...25

38. The Universe 26

39. Alone 26

40. The Listeners 27

41. Come!..29

Eugene Field (1850-1895) 30

    Biographical Sketch by Wendi Capehart 30

    01. The Rock-a-By Lady 34

    02. Garden and Cradle 35

    03. The Night Wind 35

    04. The Dinkey-Bird 37

    05. Little Blue Pigeon 39

    06. The Duel 39

    07. Good Children Street 41

    08. The Bottle Tree 42

    09. Lady Button Eyes 43

    10. The Ride to Bumpville 45

    11. Shuffle Shoon and Amber Locks 46

    12. The Shut-Eye Train 47

    13. Little Oh-Dear 49

    14. The Fly-Away Horse 50

    15. Fiddle-Dee-Dee 52

    16. The Sugar Plum Tree 53

    17. Krinken 54

    18. Pittypat and Tippytoe 56

    19. So, So, Rock-a-By, So 58

    20. Teeny-Weeny 59

    21. Buttercup, Poppy, Forget-me-not 61

22. Wynken, Blynken, and Nod 62

23. Little Mistress Sans-Merci 64

24. Hi-Spy 65

25. Little Boy Blue 66

26. Heigho, My Dearie 67

27. Fairy and Child 68

28. Child and Mother 68

29. Ganderfeather's Gift 69

30. Telling the Bees 71

31. Contentment 72

32. The Naughty Doll..74

33. Over the Hills and Far Away 75

34. Inscription for My Little Son's Silver Plate 76

35. In the Firelight..77

36. *from* Jest 'Fore Christmas 78

37. Little Homer's Slate 79

38. The Hawthorne Children 80

39. The Death of Robin Hood 82

James Whitcomb Riley (1849-1916) 85

   Biographical Sketch by Wendi Capehart.................................85

   01. When the Frost is on the Punkin...................................... 88

   02. Little Orphant Annie 89

   03. The Raggedy Man... 91

04. The Bumblebee 94

05. Granny 94

06. Our Hired Girl 96

07. A Barefoot Boy 97

08. The Old Swimmin'-Hole 98

09. There Was a Cherry-Tree 99

10. The First Bluebird 100

11. The Pixy People 101

12. On Any Ordenary Man in a High State of Laughture and Delight
.... 103

13. Pansies 103

14. The Prayer Perfect 104

15. When Early March Seems Middle May 104

16. The Funniest Thing in the World 106

17. Naughty Claude 106

18. An Impetuous Resolve 107

19. A Sudden Shower 107

20. The Man in the Moon 108

21. Craqueodoom 110

22. Prior to Miss Belle's Appearance 111

23. A Dream 113

Christina Rossetti (1830-1894) 116

Biographical Sketch by Wendi Capehart 116

01. Bread and milk for breakfast 119

02. There's snow on the fields 119

03. I dug and dug amongst the snow 119

04. Hear what the mournful linnets say 120

05. Hope is like a harebell 120

06. O wind, why do you never rest 120

07. Growing in the vale 120

08. A linnet in a gilded cage 121

09. If all were rain and never sun 121

10. O wind, where have you been 121

11. On the grassy banks 122

12. Rushes in a watery place 122

13. Heartsease in my garden bed 122

14. If I were a Queen 123

15. What are heavy? 123

16. Stroke a flint 123

17. There is but one May in the year 123

18. The summer nights are short 124

19. Twist me a crown of wind-flowers 124

20. Brown and furry 125

21. A pocket handkerchief to hem 125

22. If a pig wore a wig 126

23. Seldom "can't" 126

24. How many seconds in a minute? 126

25. What will you give me for my pound? 127

26. January cold desolate 127

27. What is pink? 128

28. Mother shake the cherry-tree 129

29. A pin has a head 129

30. Hopping frog 129

31. The city mouse 130

32. A motherless soft lambkin 130

33. When fishes set umbrellas up 131

34. The peacock has a score of eyes 131

35. Pussy has a whiskered face 131

36. In the meadow 131

37. A frisky lamb 132

38. Fly away, fly away over the sea 132

39. When the cows come home 132

40. "Ferry me across the water" 133

41. Who has seen the wind? 133

42. The horses of the sea 134

43. O sailor, come ashore 134

44. A diamond or a coal? 134

45. Boats sail on the rivers 135

46. The lily has a smooth stalk 135

47. Hurt no living thing 136

48. I caught a little ladybird 136

49. A house of cards 137

50. The rose with such a bonny blush 137

51. The peach tree on the southern wall 137

52. Is the moon tired? 138

53. If stars dropped out of heaven 138

54. If the sun could tell us half 138

55. What do the stars do 139

About AmblesideOnline 140

Introduction to the Series

Charlotte Mason said that poetry is an instructor of the conscience, and that children "must grow up upon the best… There is never a time when they are unequal to worthy thoughts, well put; inspiring tales, well told. Let Blake's 'Songs of Innocence' represent their standard in poetry…" and the result will be readers who demand the best, "the fit and beautiful expression of inspiring ideas and pictures of life" (*Parents and Children*, p. 263).

And modern research supports her claim. Researchers at the University of Liverpool found that reading poetry provides a "rocket-boost" to the brain that cannot be matched by straightforward, simple paraphrases. The research also found that poetry, in particular, "increased activity in the right hemisphere of the brain, an area concerned with 'autobiographical memory,' which helped the reader to reflect on and reappraise their own experiences in light of what they had read" (*Daily Mail*, Jan. 13, 2013).

AmblesideOnline students read a variety of poems which offer them word pictures and ideas to reflect on, and to help them interpret their own experiences.

> "[A student] should have practice, too, in reading aloud, for the most part, in the books he is using for his term's work. These should include a good deal of poetry, to accustom him to the delicate rendering of shades of meaning, and especially to make him aware that words are beautiful in themselves, that they are a source of pleasure, and are worthy of our honour; and that a beautiful word deserves to be beautifully said, with a certain roundness of tone and precision of utterance. Quite young children are open to this sort of teaching, conveyed, not in a lesson, but by a word now and then." (Charlotte Mason, *Home Education*, p. 227)

Please don't analyze and dissect these poems. There is time for that later in your young scholar's life. Just as there is a time to simply feed your young ones delicious, nourishing food, and a time later in their lives to teach them the analytical details of health, nutrition, and all about the vitamins and minerals in their food, there is a time to just read poetry and learn to enjoy it. "The thing is," Charlotte Mason said in a book she wrote for children, "to keep your eye upon words and wait to feel their force and beauty; and, when words are so fit that no other words can be put in their places, so few that none can be left out without spoiling the sense, and so fresh and musical that they delight you, then you may be sure that you are reading Literature, whether in prose or poetry. A great deal of delightful literature can be recognised only by this test." (*Ourselves Book I*, p. 41)

We hope you will enjoy reading these poems together as much as we enjoy sharing them with you.

An added note: we have tried to be sensitive to the changing language and ideas of our present day, while presenting these poems from the past as faithfully as we were able. However, it is beyond our capabilities to anticipate every new word meaning that exists or that arises in the future. We can only give the same advice and disclaimer that we would suggest for other studies, from literature through science: please preview this material, and then use it with care and discretion.

Donna-Jean Breckenridge
Lynn Bruce
Wendi Capehart
Karen Glass
Leslie Laurio
Anne White

Foreword to Volume Two by Wendi Capehart

Walter de la Mare, Eugene Field, James Whitcomb Riley, and Christina Rossetti are names which conjure magic and delight among those who are fond of poetry for children, including not a small number of children brought up in touch with their birthright of open air play, and cozy corners for dreaming over their books.

Children already think and feel most of what they will come across in these poems, only they have not yet been given the words to express those thoughts, ideas, and feelings. Give your children the benefit of the rich thought-life and strong vocabulary that comes from reading good poems. Give your entire family a rich blessing and make reading these poems part of your daily lives. Share them together, and grow together in appreciation and enjoyment of one of the finer arts.

Unconvinced? It is always hard to convince somebody who has never tried it that one's native food is delicious, but the proof is in the trying, after all. Give them a fair tasting, one bite (or one poem) a day for a season. If you struggle with them, find audio recordings and listen together. Little by little, over time, see if they don't change the way you see the world, sprinkling the everyday with the sheen of poetry.

How to Use These Poems with Young Students

It's really quite simple. Just read the poems aloud. One common approach is to read one poem a day, Monday through Thursday, and then, on Friday, ask if there are any previous poems the children would like to hear repeated.

You may also have your child read the daily poem aloud.

Or read it, casually, several times throughout the day, and see if your child doesn't start to pick up some of the poems.

Use a poem for copywork or transcription (handwriting practice).

Enjoy them. Don't dissect, analyze, parse, or otherwise drain them of their pleasure. All of those things are wonderful in their own time. But first, children (and parents) should just read lots of poems.

Walter de la Mare (1873-1956)

"Between Waking and Dreaming": Biographical Sketch by Anne White

"You must have a silver penny to get into Fairyland." (Preface to *Silver Pennies*)

"And when —after a hot breathless night during which she had lain between waking and dreaming while the lightning flared at her window, and the thunder raved over the sea —when, next morning, she came down very early to find that the hungry mice had stolen more than half of the handful of oatmeal she had left in the cupboard and that her little crock of milk had turned sour, her heart all but failed her. She sat down on the doorstep and she began to cry." ("A Penny a Day")

I read this story at about the age of eight, and it was my first meeting with Walter de la Mare, along with the poem "Some One." It's a fairy tale about a poor but generous girl and a dwarf named Moleskins who offers to help her in exchange for a penny a day…but he may not be entirely trustworthy (is he the one stealing back her pennies?). Visits to fairy grottoes are also involved. I found it a very enjoyable story, although I didn't quite understand it all. I thought it was sort of funny and sad and strange all at the same time.

Who was this writer who tried, like Moleskins, to lure young readers into his own fairy grotto? His father was a banker, and his mother was said to be related to the poet Robert Browning. He was born in the county of Kent, but had his schooling at St. Paul's Cathedral Choir School in London.

His own day job, perhaps appropriately considering his fixation on pennies, was working in the accounting department of a London oil company. He published his first short story in 1895, when he was twenty-two years old; but it was not until he was in his thirties that he received what we would now call an artist's grant, a yearly allowance from the government which allowed him to work only at writing. He experimented with stories, for both adults and children, that might be called "eerie" and "supernatural," but they were never as horrific as those of Edgar Allan Poe; they tended to be more romantic and dreamlike, involving the world of the imagination, and secret, hidden places (such as Moleskins' fairy grotto). One of his most famous poems, "The Listeners," combines all of these elements:

> 'Is there anybody there?' said the Traveller,
>
> Knocking on the moonlit door;
>
> And his horse in the silence champed the grasses
>
> Of the forest's ferny floor…
>
> But no one descended to the Traveller;
>
> No head from the leaf-fringed sill
>
> Leaned over and looked into his grey eyes,
>
> Where he stood perplexed and still.

Walter de la Mare married and had four children, one of whom became a publisher and published his father's books.

He received various types of official recognition for his poems and stories, such as the Order of the Companions of Honour in 1948 and the Order of Merit in 1953. He died in 1958 and is buried in St. Paul's Cathedral. The English writer Thomas Hardy admired his poetry so much that, a few days before he died (in 1928), Hardy asked his wife to read him "The Listeners," and afterwards said, "That is possibly the finest poem of the century."

> Words may create rare images
>
> Within their narrow bound;
>
> 'Twas speechless childhood brought me these,
>
> As music may, in sound. ("The Burning-glass")

01. The Horseman

I heard a horseman
    Ride over the hill;
The moon shone clear,
    The night was still;
His helm was silver,
    And pale was he;
And the horse he rode
    Was of ivory.

02. Up and Down

Down the Hill of Ludgate,
    Up the Hill of Fleet,
To and fro and East and West
    With people flows the street;
Even the King of England
    On Temple Bar must beat
For leave to ride to Ludgate
    Down the Hill of Fleet.

03. Mrs. Earth

Mrs. Earth makes silver black,
    Mrs. Earth makes iron red
But Mrs. Earth can not stain gold,
    Nor ruby red.
Mrs. Earth the slenderest bone
    Whitens in her bosom cold,
But Mrs. Earth can change my dreams
    No more than ruby or gold.

Mrs. Earth and Mr. Sun
    Can tan my skin, and tire my toes,
But all that I'm thinking of, ever shall think,
    Why, either knows.

04. Tired Tim

Poor Tired Tim! It's sad for him.
He lags the long bright morning through,
Ever so tired of nothing to do;
He moons and mopes the livelong day,
Nothing to think about, nothing to say;
Up to bed with his candle to creep,
Too tired to yawn, too tired to sleep:
Poor Tired Tim! It's sad for him.

05. I Can't Abear

I can't abear a Butcher,
    I can't abide his meat,
The ugliest shop of all is his,
    The ugliest in the street;
Bakers' are warm, cobblers' dark,
    Chemists' burn watery lights;
But oh, the sawdust butcher's shop,
    That ugliest of sights!

06. Some One

Some one came knocking
    At my wee, small door;
Some one came knocking,
    I'm sure–sure–sure;
I listened, I opened,

I looked to left and right,
But naught there was a-stirring
   In the still dark night;
Only the busy beetle
   Tap-tapping in the wall,
Only from the forest
   The screech-owl's call,
Only the cricket whistling
   While the dewdrops fall,
So I know not who came knocking,
   At all, at all, at all.

07. The Little Bird

My dear Daddie bought a mansion
   For to bring my Mammie to,
In a hat with a long feather,
   And a trailing gown of blue;
And a company of fiddlers
   And a rout of maids and men
Danced the clock round to the morning,
   In a gay house-warming then.
And when all the guests were gone, and
   All was still as still can be,
In from the dark ivy hopped a
   Wee small bird: and that was Me.

08. The Cupboard

I know a little cupboard,
   With a teeny tiny key,
And there's a jar of Lollypops
     For me, me, me.

It has a little shelf, my dear,
    As dark as dark can be,
And there's a dish of Banbury Cakes
      For me, me, me.

I have a small fat grandmamma,
    With a very slippery knee,
And she's the Keeper of the Cupboard
      With the key, key, key.

And when I'm very good, my dear,
    As good as good can be,
There's Banbury Cakes, and Lollypops
      For me, me, me.

09. Hide and Seek

Hide and seek, says the Wind,
    In the shade of the woods;
Hide and seek, says the Moon,
    To the hazel buds;
Hide and seek, says the Cloud,
    Star on to star;
Hide and seek, says the Wave,
    At the harbour bar;
Hide and seek, say I,
    To myself, and step
Out of the dream of Wake
    Into the dream of Sleep.

10. The Window

Behind the blinds I sit and watch
    The people passing —passing by;
And not a single one can see
    My tiny watching eye.

They cannot see my little room,
    All yellowed with the shaded sun;
They do not even know I'm here;
    Nor'll guess when I am gone.

11. A Widow's Weeds

"Widow's weeds" means black mourning clothes; but in this poem it has a double meaning.

A poor old Widow in her weeds
Sowed her garden with wild-flower seeds;
Not too shallow, and not too deep,
And down came April–drip–drip–drip.
Up shone May, like gold, and soon
Green as an arbour grew leafy June.
And now all summer she sits and sews
Where willow herb, comfrey, bugloss blows,
Teasle and pansy, meadowsweet,
Campion, toadflax, and rough hawksbit;
Brown bee orchis, and Peals of Bells;
Clover, burnet, and thyme she smells;
Like Oberon's meadows her garden is
Drowsy from dawn to dusk with bees.
Weeps she never, but sometimes sighs,
And peeps at her garden with bright brown eyes;

And all she has is all she needs —
A poor Old Widow in her weeds.

12. The Little Green Orchard

Some one is always sitting there,
    In the little green orchard;
  Even when the sun is high
  In noon's unclouded sky,
  And faintly droning goes
  The bee from rose to rose,
Some one in shadow is sitting there
    In the little green orchard.

Yes, when the twilight's falling softly
    In the little green orchard;
  When the grey dew distills
  And every flower-cup fills;
  When the last blackbird says,
  'What —what!' and goes her way —ssh!
I have heard voices calling softly
    In the little green orchard.

Not that I am afraid of being there,
    In the little green orchard;
  Why, when the moon's been bright,
  Shedding her lonesome light,
  And moths like ghosties come,
  And the horned snail leaves home:
I've sat there, whispering and listening there,
    In the little green orchard.

Only it's strange to be feeling there,
    In the little green orchard;
Whether you paint or draw,
Dig, hammer, chop or saw;
When you are most alone,
All but the silence gone . . .
Some one is watching and waiting there,
    In the little green orchard.

13. King David

King David was a sorrowful man:
    No cause for his sorrow had he;
And he called for the music of a hundred harps,
    To ease his melancholy.

They played till they all fell silent:
    Played —and play sweet did they;
But the sorrow that haunted the heart of King David
    They could not charm away.

He rose; and in his garden
    Walked by the moon alone,
A nightingale hidden in a cypress-tree
    Jargoned on and on.

King David lifted his sad eyes
    Into the dark-boughed tree —
"Tell me, thou little bird that singest,
    Who taught my grief to thee?"

But the bird in no wise heeded
    And the king in the cool of the moon

Hearkened to the nightingale's sorrowfulness,
    Till all his own was gone.

14. The Old House

A very, very old house I know —
And ever so many people go,
Past the small lodge, forlorn and still,
Under the heavy branches, till
Comes the blank wall, and there's the door.
Go in they do; come out no more.
No voice says aught; no spark of light
Across that threshold cheers the sight;
Only the evening star on high
Less lonely makes a lonely sky,
As, one by one, the people go
Into that very old house I know.

15. Unstooping

Low on his fours the Lion
    Treads with the surly Bear;
But Men straight upward from the dust
    Walk with their heads in air;
The free sweet winds of heaven,
    The sunlight from on high
Beat on their clear bright cheeks and brows
    As they go striding by;
The doors of all their houses
    They arch so they may go,
Uplifted o'er the four-foot beasts,
    Unstooping, to and fro.

16. All but Blind

All but blind
   In his chambered hole
Gropes for worms
   The four-clawed Mole.
All but blind
   In the evening sky
The hooded Bat
   Twirls softly by.
All but blind
   In the burning day
The Barn-Owl blunders
   On her way.
And blind as are
   These three to me,
So blind to someone
   I must be.

17. Nicholas Nye

Thistle and darnell and dock grew there,
   And a bush, in the corner, of may,
On the orchard wall I used to sprawl
   In the blazing heat of the day;
Half asleep and half awake,
   While the birds went twittering by,
And nobody there my lone to share
    But Nicholas Nye.

Nicholas Nye was lean and gray,
   Lame of leg and old,

More than a score of donkey's years
    He had been since he was foaled;
He munched the thistles, purple and spiked,
    Would sometimes stoop and sigh,
And turn to his head, as if he said,
    "Poor Nicholas Nye!"

Alone with his shadow he'd drowse in the meadow,
    Lazily swinging his tail,
At break of day he used to bray, —
    Not much too hearty and hale;
But a wonderful gumption was under his skin,
    And a clean calm light in his eye,
And once in a while; he'd smile: —
    Would Nicholas Nye.

Seem to be smiling at me, he would,
    From his bush in the corner, of may, —
Bony and ownerless, widowed and worn,
    Knobble-kneed, lonely and gray;
And over the grass would seem to pass
    'Neath the deep dark blue of the sky,
Something much better than words between me
    And Nicholas Nye.

But dusk would come in the apple boughs,
    The green of the glow-worm shine,
The birds in nest would crouch to rest,
    And home I'd trudge to mine;
And there, in the moonlight, dark with dew,
    Asking not wherefore nor why,
Would brood like a ghost, and as still as a post,
    Old Nicholas Nye.

18. Five Eyes

In Hans' old Mill his three black cats
Watch the bins for the thieving rats.
Whisker and claw, they crouch in the night,
Their five eyes smouldering green and bright:
Squeaks from the flour sacks, squeaks from where
The cold wind stirs on the empty stair,
Squeaking and scampering, everywhere.
Then down they pounce, now in, now out,
At whisking tail, and sniffing snout;
While lean old Hans he snores away
Till peep of light at break of day;
Then up he climbs to his creaking mill,
Out come his cats all grey with meal —
Jekkel, and Jessup, and one-eyed Jill.

19. Summer Evening

The sandy cat by the Farmer's chair
Mews at his knee for dainty fare;
Old Rover in his moss-greened house
Mumbles a bone, and barks at a mouse
In the dewy fields the cattle lie
Chewing the cud 'neath a fading sky
Dobbin at manger pulls his hay:
Gone is another summer's day.

20. Earth Folk

The cat she walks on padded claws,
The wolf on the hills lays stealthy paws,

Feathered birds in the rain-sweet sky
At their ease in the air, flit low, flit high.

The oak's blind, tender roots pierce deep,
His green crest towers, dimmed in sleep,
Under the stars whose thrones are set
Where never prince hath journeyed yet.

21. The Ruin

When the last colours of the day
Have from their burning ebbed away,
About that ruin, cold and lone,
The cricket shrills from stone to stone;
And scattering o'er its darkened green,
Bands of the fairies may be seen,
Chattering like grasshoppers, their feet
Dancing a thistledown dance round it:
While the great gold of the mild moon
Tinges their tiny acorn shoon.

22. Trees

Of all the trees in England,
   Her sweet three corners in,
Only the Ash, the bonnie Ash
   Burns fierce while it is green.

Of all the trees in England,
   From sea to sea again,
The Willow loveliest stoops her boughs
   Beneath the driving rain.

Of all the trees in England,
   Past frankincense and myrrh,
There's none for smell, of bloom and smoke,
   Like Lime and Juniper.

Of all the trees in England,
   Oak, Elder, Elm and Thorn,
The Yew alone burns lamps of peace
   For them that lie forlorn.

23. Silver

Slowly, silently, now the moon
Walks the night in her silver shoon:
This way, and that, she peers and sees
Silver fruit upon silver trees;
One by one the casements catch
Her beams beneath the silvery thatch;
Couched in his kennel, like a log,
With paws of silver sleeps the dog
From their shadowy cote the white breasts peep
Of doves in a silver-feathered sleep;
A harvest mouse goes scampering by,
With silver claws and silver eye;
And moveless fish in the water gleam
By silver reeds in a silver stream.

24. Nobody Knows

Often I've heard the Wind sigh
    By the ivied orchard wall,
Over the leaves in the dark night,
    Breathe a sighing call,
And faint away in the silence
    While I, in my bed,
Wondered, 'twixt dreaming and waking,
    What it said.

Nobody knows what the Wind is,
    Under the height of the sky,
Where the hosts of the stars keep far away house
    And its wave sweeps by —
Just a great wave of the air,
    Tossing the leaves in its sea,
And foaming under the eaves of the roof
    That covers me.

And so we live under deep water,
    All of us, beasts and men,
And our bodies are buried down under the sand,
    When we go again;
And leave, like the fishes, our shells,
    And float on the Wind and away,
To where, o'er the marvellous tides of the air,
    Burns day.

25. Wanderers

Wide are the meadows of night,
    And daisies are shining there,
Tossing their lovely dews,
    Lustrous and fair;
And through these sweet fields go,
    Wanderers amid the stars —
Venus, Mercury, Uranus, Neptune,
    Saturn, Jupiter, Mars.

'Tired in their silver, they move,
    And circling, whisper and say,
Fair are the blossoming meads of delight
    Through which we stray.

26. Many a Mickle

A little sound —
    Only a little, a little —
The breath in a reed,
    A trembling fiddle;
A trumpet's ring,
    The shuddering drum;
So all the glory, bravery, hush
    Of music come.
A little sound —
    Only a stir and a sigh
Of each green leaf
    Its fluttering neighbor by;
Oak on to oak,
    The wide dark forest through —

So o'er the watery wheeling world
    The night winds go.
A little sound,
    Only a little, a little —
The thin high drone
    Of the simmering kettle,
The gathering frost,
    The click of needle and thread;
Mother, the fading wall, the dream,
    The drowsy bed.

27. Will Ever?

Will he ever be weary of wandering,
    The flaming sun?
Ever weary of waning in lovelight,
    The white still moon?
Will ever a shepherd come
    With a crook of simple gold,
And lead all the little stars
    Like lambs to the fold?

Will ever the Wanderer sail
    From over the sea,
Up the river of water,
    To the stones to me?
Will he take us all into his ship,
    Dreaming, and waft us far,
To where in the clouds of the West
    The Islands are?

28. The Song of the Secret

Where is beauty?
   Gone, gone:
The cold winds have taken it
  With their faint moan;
The white stars have shaken it,
  Trembling down,
Into the pathless deeps of the sea.
   Gone, gone
 Is beauty from me.
The clear naked flower
 Is faded and dead;
The green-leafed willow,
  Drooping her head,
Whispers low to the shade
  Of her boughs in the stream,
   Sighing a beauty,
   Secret as dream.

29. The Song of the Soldiers

As I sat musing by the frozen dyke,
There was a man marching with a bright steel pike,
Marching in the dayshine like a ghost came he,
And behind me was the moaning and the murmur
  Of the sea.

As I sat musing, 'twas not one but ten —
Rank on rank of ghostly soldiers marching o'er the fen,
Marching in the misty air they showed in dreams to me,
And behind me was the shouting and the shattering
  of the sea.

As I sat musing, 'twas a host in dark array,
With their horses and their cannon wheeling onward
    to the fray,
Moving like a shadow to the fate the brave must dree,
And behind me roared the drums, rang the trumpets
    Of the sea.

30. The Bees' Song

Thousandz of thornz there be
On the Rozez where gozes
The Zebra of Zee:
Sleek, striped, and hairy,
The steed of the Fairy
Princess of Zee.

Heavy with blossomz be
The Rozez that growzez
In the thickets of Zee.
Where grazez the Zebra,
Marked Abracadeeebra,
Of the Princess of Zee.

And he nozez that poziez
Of the Rozez that grozez
So luvez'm and free,
With an eye, dark and wary,
In search of a Fairy,
Whose Rozez he knowzez
Were not honeyed for he,
But to breathe a sweet incense

To solace the Princess
Of far-away Zee.

31. Song of Enchantment

"Widdershins" means counterclockwise. Going around something widdershins is said to cause bad luck.

A Song of Enchantment I sang me there,
In a green-green wood, by waters fair,
Just as the words came up to me
I sang it under the wildwood tree.

Widdershins turned I, singing it low,
Watching the wild birds come and go;
No cloud in the deep dark blue to be seen
Under the thick-thatched branches green.

Twilight came; silence came;
The planet of Evening's silver flame;
By darkening paths I wandered through
Thickets trembling with drops of dew.

But the music is lost and the words are gone
Of the song I sang as I sat alone,
Ages and ages have fallen on me —
On the wood and the pool and the elder tree.

32. Dream Song

  Sunlight, moonlight,
    Twilight, starlight —
Gloaming at the close of day,
    And an owl calling,

 Cool dews falling
In a wood of oak and may.

 Lantern-light, taper-light,
  Torchlight, no-light:
Darkness at the shut of day,
  And lions roaring,
  Their wrath pouring
In wild waste places far away.

 Elf-light, bat-light,
  Touchwood-light and toad-light,
And the sea a shimmering gloom of grey,
  And a small face smiling
  In a dream's beguiling
In a world of wonders far away.

33. The Song of Shadows

Sweep thy faint Strings, Musician,
 With thy long lean hand;
Downward the starry tapers burn,
 Sinks soft the waning sand;
The old hound whimpers couched in sleep,
 The embers smoulder low;
Across the walls the shadows
  Come, and go.

Sweep softly thy strings, Musician,
 The minutes mount to hours;
Frost on the windless casement weaves
 A labyrinth of flowers;
Ghosts linger in the darkening air,

Hearken at the open door;
Music hath called them, dreaming,
    Home once more.

34. The Song of the Mad Prince

Who said, 'Peacock Pie?'
    The old King to the sparrow:
Who said, 'Crops are ripe?'
    Rust to the harrow:
Who said, 'Where sleeps she now?'
    Where rests she now her head,
Bathed in eve's loveliness'? —
    That's what I said.

Who said, 'Ay, mum's the word'?
    Sexton to willow:
Who said, 'Green duck for dreams,
    Moss for a pillow'?

Who said, 'All Time's delight
    Hath she for narrow bed;
Life's troubled bubble broken'? —
    That's what I said.

35. The Song of Finis

At the edge of All the Ages
    A Knight sate on his steed,
His armor red and thin with rust
    His soul from sorrow freed;
And he lifted up his visor
    From a face of skin and bone,

And his horse turned head and whinnied
    As the twain stood there alone.

No bird above that steep of time
    Sang of a livelong quest;
No wind breathed,
    Rest:
"Lone for an end!" cried Knight to steed,
    Loosed an eager rein —
Charged with his challenge into space:
    And quiet did quiet remain.

36. November (also called Autumn)

from *Poems*, 1906

There is wind where the rose was,
Cold rain where sweet grass was,
And clouds like sheep
Stream o'er the steep
Grey skies where the lark was.

Nought warm where your hand was,
Nought gold where your hair was,
But phantom, forlorn,
Beneath the thorn,
Your ghost where your face was.

Cold wind where your voice was,
Tears, tears where my heart was,
And ever with me,
Child, ever with me,
Silence where hope was.

37. The Scribe

from *Collected Poems, 1901-1918*, 1920

What lovely things
    Thy hand hath made:
The smooth-plumed bird
    In its emerald shade,
The seed of the grass,
    The speck of the stone
Which the wayfaring ant
    Stirs —and hastes on!

Though I should sit
    By some tarn in thy hills,
Using its ink
    As the spirit wills
To write of Earth's wonders,
    Its live, willed things,
Flit would the ages
    On soundless wings
Ere unto Z
    My pen drew nigh
Leviathan told,
    And the honey-fly:
And still would remain
    My wit to try —
My worn reeds broken,
    The dark tarn dry,
All words forgotten —
    Thou, Lord, and I.

38. The Universe

from *Collected Poems, 1901-1918*, 1920

I heard a little child beneath the stars
    Talk as he ran along
To some sweet riddle in his mind that seemed
    A-tiptoe into song.

In his dark eyes lay a wild universe, —
    Wild forests, peaks, and crests;
Angels and fairies, giants, wolves and he
    Were that world's only guests.

Elsewhere was home and mother, his warm bed: —
    Now, only God alone
Could, armed with all His power and wisdom, make
    Earths richer than his own.

O Man!–thy dreams, thy passions, hopes, desires!–
    He in his pity keep
A homely bed where love may lull a child's
    Fond Universe asleep!

39. Alone

from *The Listeners*, 1916

A very old woman
Lives in yon house —
The squeak of the cricket,
The stir of the mouse,

Are all she knows
Of the earth and us.

Once she was young,
Would dance and play,
Like many another
Young popinjay;
And run to her mother
At dusk of day.

And colours bright
She delighted in;
The fiddle to hear,
And to lift her chin,
And sing as small
As a twittering wren.

But age apace
Comes at last to all;
And a lone house filled
With the cricket's call;
And the scampering mouse
In the hollow wall.

40. The Listeners

from *The Listeners*, 1916

'Is there anybody there?' said the Traveller,
    Knocking on the moonlit door;
And his horse in the silence champed the grasses
    Of the forest's ferny floor:
And a bird flew up out of the turret,

Above the Traveller's head:
And he smote upon the door again a second time;
   'Is there anybody there?' he said.
But no one descended to the Traveller;
   No head from the leaf-fringed sill
Leaned over and looked into his grey eyes,
   Where he stood perplexed and still.
But only a host of phantom listeners
   That dwelt in the lone house then
Stood listening in the quiet of the moonlight
   To that voice from the world of men:
Stood thronging the faint moonbeams on the dark stair,
   That goes down to the empty hall,
Hearkening in an air stirred and shaken
   By the lonely Traveller's call.
And he felt in his heart their strangeness,
   Their stillness answering his cry,
While his horse moved, cropping the dark turf,
   'Neath the starred and leafy sky;
For he suddenly smote on the door, even
   Louder, and lifted his head: —
'Tell them I came, and no one answered,
   That I kept my word,' he said.
Never the least stir made the listeners,
   Though every word he spake
Fell echoing through the shadowiness of the still house
   From the one man left awake:
Ay, they heard his foot upon the stirrup,
   And the sound of iron on stone,
And how the silence surged softly backward,
   When the plunging hoofs were gone.

41. Come!

from *Poems*, 1906

From an island of the sea
Sounds a voice that summons me, —
"Turn thy prow, sailor, come
    With the wind home!"

Sweet o'er the rainbow foam,
Sweet in the treetops, "Come,
Coral, cliff, and watery sand,
    Sea-wave to land!

"Droop not thy lids at night,
Furl not thy sails from flight! . . ."
Cease, cease, above the wave,
    Deep as the grave!

O, what voice of the salt sea
Calls me so insistently?
Echoes, echoes, night and day, —
    "Come, come away!"

Eugene Field (1850-1895)

Biographical Sketch by Wendi Capehart

When I was a young child, sometimes my father would not pay our electricity bill and the power would go out. My mother didn't want us to worry, so she would tell us she turned the power off on purpose and it was a popcorn party night. We would pop popcorn on the gas stove, and sit in a room lit by candles, eating popcorn, telling stories, and sometimes reciting poems. Usually they would be the poems of James Whitcomb Riley, but sometimes we heard some of Eugene Field's poems, too. "Wynken, Blynken, and Nod" was a favourite, often recited as the candles were blown out and we were sent to bed.

Eugene Field was born in Missouri in 1850, and lived there until he was six years old, when his mother died. His father was a busy lawyer who was part of a team of lawyers working on an very important legal case in America's history. Dred and Harriet Scott, Black Americans held in slavery, had sued the courts for their freedom. The case took ten years to work through the courts, and the lawyers who took their case agreed to work on it for free. The case had already been going on for eight or nine years when Eugene's mother died.

Unable to care for the boys by himself, Roswell Field sent Eugene and his brother Roswell to Vermont to be reared by their older spinster cousin and her mother. They were strict but loving, and he was fond of them, but of course, he deeply missed his mother and felt that separation all his life.

Puritan New England and Eugene, a free spirited lad who liked to play practical jokes and thought of himself as the grasshopper of Aesop's fable, often clashed. But when he grew up Eugene admitted that he was grateful to New England and his relatives for "pounding me with the Bible and the Spelling-Book."

Eugene did not do well in school, so his cousins sent him to Mr. Tufts, a private tutor who ran a small boys' school. Mr. Tufts was a very forgiving man. He did not expel Eugene, even when Eugene egged the boys on to build a fort with a hidden moat around it. He then got Mr. Tufts to chase them to their secret fortress so he would fall in, nearly neck deep in mud and muck.

Eugene Field

Eugene did not do well at college. His father died, and he dropped out. Then he tried two more colleges, but he would rather play pranks than study. He painted the college president's house in the college colours, and he set off the school cannons at midnight, and finally gave up college altogether. He used some of his inheritance to travel Europe with a close friend (who would become his brother-in-law). They played and had a grand time, buying bits of art and souvenirs that they then had to sell in order to have enough money to return home again after six months, with a poodle named McSweeney! His brother, Roswell, was able to live for seven years on the same amount Eugene had squandered in six months. But sometimes, Roswell said, he thought Eugene had been the wiser of the two after all.

Eugene finally found work as a journalist. He married Julia, his friend's little sister, and for the rest of their lives, Eugene had all of his employers send the money he earned directly to Julia, because he knew he would spend it unwisely. They loved each other dearly, and had eight children together. Two died in infancy, and their oldest child died at thirteen.

Field was not a very good journalist. He liked to fix up his stories so they would be more amusing and more interesting. He was a good opinion writer and columnist for the same reason that he was a poor journalist. He knew how to write in ways that amused his readers, while often making sharp points hidden beneath the humour. He worked as an editor and columnist for several newspapers in the Midwest, until he moved to Chicago and worked for a paper there until his death.

He loved to read, and among his favourite books even as an adult included a book of stories about King Arthur, an old book of English ballads, Marco Polo's *Travels*, several collections of fairy tales, including those by the Grimm brothers, and Hans Christian Andersen's stories. He thought that reading good books made him a better writer.

He never stopped playing practical jokes. There were only two chairs in his office. One was his own, the other was large wooden chair which had no bottom. He would toss a pillow or blanket over the spot where a seat might be and visitors would find themselves suddenly sprawling as they sat down and fell partway through the chair.

In the newspaper office where he worked in Chicago, it was his custom to leave a pair of slippers in his office. When he arrived at work he removed his jacket and shoes, rolled up his pant legs and sleeves, loosened his suspenders, put on his slippers, and propped his feet up his desk to write, using his knees for a writing desk. This sounds only mildly eccentric to us, but to his contemporaries it was bewildering. Remember that dress was very conventional at this time.

He loved to compose in colored inks. In those times, colored inks were used in ink pots, and most people who switched colours would use a new pen for each new colour. Field preferred to use his ancient flannel coat as a pen-wiper, so it was dabbled all over with streaks of brightly colored ink. One of his co-workers called it his Joseph's coat.

He published a book he called *The New England Primer*, in which he gave such advice as telling children to pat the wasp, eat wormy apples, put mud in the baby's ears, and play certain pranks on their father (pranks which, the author intimated, might make it a question as to when the children would again eat their meals sitting down).

He liked to make rude, startling, or scary faces at children when he thought no adults were looking.

He began publishing his poetry only after he became a successful newspaper editor and columnist.

It is odd to think that a man who made faces at children to make them cry was known for such seemingly sentimental poetry as "Little Boy Blue," and was called the "Children's Poet"; but others have pointed out that his most sentimental poems are really from a parent's point of view, not the child's. Some people think that in his most sentimental poems we can see the heart of a boy who never got over missing his mother.

He had always liked to play with words, making up new ones, creating silly ballads and rhymes about his friends, and about the men who came to court his sisters-in-law. He had always been a man of whimsical ides, and half a child himself. Poetry was an outlet for his wordplay and whimsy. It was also a way to support his family after his death, because he had learned he would probably not live to see all his children grow up.

Field buckled down to work and wrote and published several books in a row. And, like other poets of the time, such as Dunbar and Riley, at last he succumbed to entreaties to perform for pay on the public speaking platform. It was exhausting, but he made more money from one performance than he did from several columns.

He continued to write his columns as well, but he worked less often at the office. He would write his columns from home, and then send his son into town to deliver them at the newspaper office.

Eugene Field died at his home on Lake Michigan in early November, 1895. He was forty-five years old. He left behind his wife and five surviving children, two of whom were not much more than babies. He was so beloved by so many, that they had to be turned away from the funeral, and the church building was filled to capacity.

He had once said he really did not love all children, just his own. Yet in the last period of his life, often in the evenings the neighborhood children would gather in his yard and he would entertain them with fanciful stories of marvelous creatures which resembled, at first, the birds, crickets, and other inhabitants of local woods and gardens. But his creatures were creatures of the imagination, his descriptions included real words nobody else would have used with children, and brand new words nobody had heard before because he made them up. You will find words like these in his poetry, too. It doesn't matter. You don't have to know precisely what they all mean. American writer and book-seller Denise Chávez wrote an essay about her childhood among books and stories in which she mentions the poem "The Dinkey-Bird." She says that "I never knew what an amfalula tree was, and yet I did. I knew other, brighter and better worlds existed out there — worlds imagined and longed for."

Eugene Field's poems are poems of childhood, children, love, laughter, loss, and imagination. Let them give you glimmerings of imagined worlds of your own.

Poems from *Lullaby-Land* (1896)

01. The Rock-a-By Lady

Poppies are often associated with sleep in poems and stories.

The Rock-a-By Lady from Hushaby street
    Comes stealing; comes creeping;
The poppies they hang from her head to her feet,
And each hath a dream that is tiny and fleet
She bringeth her poppies to you, my sweet,
    When she findeth you sleeping!
There is one little dream of a beautiful drum
    "Rub-a-dub!" it goeth;
There is one little dream of a big sugar-plum,
And lo! thick and fast the other dreams come
Of popguns that bang, and tin tops that hum,
    And a trumpet that bloweth!
And dollies peep out of those wee little dreams
    With laughter and singing;
And boats go a-floating on silvery streams,
And the stars peek-a-boo with their own misty gleams,
And up, up, and up, where the Mother Moon beams,
    The fairies go winging!
Would you dream all these dreams that are tiny and fleet?
    They'll come to you sleeping;
So shut the two eyes that are weary, my sweet,
For the Rock-a-By Lady from Hushaby street,
With poppies that hang from her head to her feet,
    Comes stealing; comes creeping.

02. Garden and Cradle

When our babe he goeth walking in his garden,
    Around his tinkling feet the sunbeams play;
      The posies they are good to him,
      And bow them as they should to him,
    As fareth he upon his kingly way;
      And birdlings of the wood to him
    Make music, gentle music, all the day,
When our babe he goeth walking in his garden.

When our babe he goeth swinging in his cradle,
    Then the night it looketh ever sweetly down;
      The little stars are kind to him,
      The moon she hath a mind to him
    And layeth on his head a golden crown;
      And singeth then the wind to him
    A song, the gentle song of Bethle'm-town,
When our babe he goeth swinging in his cradle.

03. The Night Wind

Have you ever heard the wind go "Yoooooo"?
'Tis a pitiful sound to hear!
It seems to chill you through and through
With a strange and speechless fear.
'Tis the voice of the night that broods outside
When folks should be asleep,
And many and many's the time I've cried
To the darkness brooding far and wide
Over the land and the deep:
"Whom do you want, O lonely night,
That you wail the long hours through?"

And the night would say in its ghostly way:
    "Yoooooooo!
    Yoooooooo!
    Yoooooooo!"

Mother told me long ago
  (When I was a little tad)
That when the night went wailing so,
  Somebody had been bad;
Then, when I was snug in bed,
  Whither I had been sent,
With the blankets pulled up round my head,
I'd think of what my mother'd said,
  And wonder what boy she meant!
And "Who's been bad today?" I'd ask
  Of the wind that hoarsely blew,
And the voice would say in its meaningful way.
    "Yoooooooo!
    Yoooooooo!
    Yoooooooo!"

That this was true I must allow
  You'll not believe it, though!
Yes, though I'm quite a model now,
  I was not always so.
And if you doubt what things I say,
  Suppose you make the test;
Suppose, when you've been bad some day
And up to bed are sent away
  From mother and the rest
Suppose you ask, "Who has been bad?"
  And then you'll hear what's true;
For the wind will moan in its ruefulest tone:

"Yooooooo!
Yooooooo!
Yooooooo!"

04. The Dinkey-Bird

Bravuras, staccatos, roulades, appoggiaturas, robustos, and roundelay are all terms related to different types of songs and music.

In an ocean, 'way out yonder
    (As all sapient people know),
Is the land of Wonder-Wander,
    Whither children love to go;
It's their playing, romping, swinging,
    That give great joy to me
While the Dinkey-Bird goes singing
    In the amfalula tree!

There the gum-drops grow like cherries,
    And taffy's thick as peas —
Caramels you pick like berries
    When, and where, and how you please;
Big red sugar-plums are clinging
    To the cliffs beside that sea
Where the Dinkey-Bird is singing
    In the amfalula tree.

So when children shout and scamper
    And make merry all the day,
When there's naught to put a damper
    To the ardor of their play;
When I hear their laughter ringing,
    Then I'm sure as sure can be

That the Dinkey-Bird is singing
    In the amfalula tree.

For the Dinkey-Bird's bravuras
    And staccatos are so sweet —
His roulades, appoggiaturas,
    And robustos so complete,
That the youth of every nation —
    Be they near or far away —
Have especial delectation
    In that gladsome roundelay.

Their eyes grow bright and brighter,
    Their lungs begin to crow,
Their hearts get light and lighter,
    And their cheeks are all aglow;
For an echo cometh bringing
    The news to all and me,
That the Dinkey-Bird is singing
    In the amfalula tree.

I'm sure you like to go there
    To see your feathered friend —
And so many goodies grow there
    You would like to comprehend!
Speed, little dreams, your winging
    To that land across the sea
Where the Dinkey-Bird is singing
    In the amfalula tree!

05. Little Blue Pigeon

Sleep, little pigeon, and fold your wings —
    Little blue pigeon with velvet eyes;
Sleep to the singing of mother-bird swinging —
    Swinging the nest where her little one lies.

Away out yonder I see a star —
    Silvery star with a tinkling song;
To the soft dew falling I hear it calling —
    Calling and tinkling the night along.

In through the window a moonbeam comes —
    Little gold moonbeam with misty wings;
All silently creeping, it asks: "Is he sleeping —
    Sleeping and dreaming while mother sings?"

Up from the sea there floats the sob
    Of the waves that are breaking upon the shore,
As though they were groaning in anguish, and moaning —
    Bemoaning the ship that shall come no more.

But sleep, little pigeon, and fold your wings —
    Little blue pigeon with mournful eyes;
Am I not singing?? —see, I am swinging —
    Swinging the nest where my darling lies.

06. The Duel

The gingham dog and the calico cat
Side by side on the table sat;
'Twas half-past twelve, and (what do you think!)
Nor one nor the other had slept a wink!

The old Dutch clock and the Chinese plate
　Appeared to know as sure as fate
There was going to be a terrible spat.
　　(I wasn't there; I simply state
　　What was told me by the Chinese plate!)

The gingham dog went "bow-wow-wow!"
And the calico cat replied "mee-ow!"
The air was littered, an hour or so,
With bits of gingham and calico,
　　While the old Dutch clock in place
　　Up with its hands before its face,
For it always dreaded a family row!
　　(Now mind: I'm only telling you
　　What the old Dutch clock declares is true!)

The Chinese plate looked very blue,
And wailed, "Oh, dear! what shall we do?"
But the gingham dog and the calico cat
Wallowed this way and tumbled that,
　　Employing every tooth and claw
　　In the awfullest way you ever saw--
And, oh! how the gingham and calico flew!
　　(Don't fancy I exaggerate!
　　I got my news from the Chinese plate!)

Next morning, where the two had sat,
They found no trace of dog or cat;
And some folks think unto this day
That burglars stole that pair away!
　　But the truth about the cat and pup
　　Is this: they ate each other up!
Now what do you really think of that!

(The old Dutch clock it told me so,
And that is how I came to know.)

07. Good Children Street

There's a dear little home in Good-Children street —
    My heart turneth fondly to-day
Where tinkle of tongues and patter of feet
    Make sweetest of music at play;
Where the sunshine of love illumines each face
And warms every heart in that old-fashioned place.

For dear little children go romping about
    With dollies and tin tops and drums,
And, my! how they frolic and scamper and shout
    Till bedtime too speedily comes!
Oh, days they are golden and days they are fleet
With little folk living in Good-Children street.

See, here comes an army with gulls painted red,
    And swords, caps, and plumes of all sorts;
The captain rides gaily and proudly ahead
    On a stick-horse that prances and snorts!
Oh, legions of soldiers you're certain to meet —
Nice make-believe soldiers —in Good-Children street.

And yonder Odette wheels her dolly about —
    Poor dolly! I'm sure she is ill,
For one of her blue china eyes has dropped out
    And her voice is asthmatic'ly shrill.
Then, too, I observe she is minus her feet,
Which causes much sorrow in Good-Children street.

'Tis so the dear children go romping about
    With dollies and banners and drums,
And I venture to say they are sadly put out
    When an end to their jollity comes:
Oh, days they are golden and days they are fleet
With little folk living in Good-Children street!

08. The Bottle Tree

A bottle tree bloometh in Winkyway land —
    Heigh-ho for a bottle, I say!
A snug little berth in that ship I demand
    That rocketh the Bottle-Tree babies away
    Where the Bottle Tree bloometh by night and by day
And reacheth its fruit to each wee, dimpled hand;
    You take of that fruit as much as you list,
    For colic's a nuisance that doesn't exist!
So cuddle me close, and cuddle me fast,
    And cuddle me snug in my cradle away,
For I hunger and thirst for that precious repast —
    Heigh-ho for a bottle, I say!

The Bottle Tree bloometh by night and by day!
    Heigh-ho for Winkyway land!
And Bottle-Tree fruit (as I've heard people say)
    Makes bellies of Bottle-Tree babies expand —
    And that is a trick I would fain understand!
Heigh-ho for a bottle to-day!
    And heigh-ho for a bottle to-night!
    A bottle of milk that is creamy and white!
So cuddle me close, and cuddle me fast,
    And cuddle me snug in my cradle away,

For I hunger and thirst for that precious repast —
    Heigh-ho for a bottle, I say!

09. Lady Button Eyes

"Dight" means clothed, and "raiment" is clothing.

When the busy day is done,
And my weary little one
Rocketh gently to and fro;
When the night winds softly blow,
And the crickets in the glen
Chirp and chirp and chirp again;
When upon the haunted green
Fairies dance around their queen —
Then from yonder misty skies
Cometh Lady Button-Eyes.

Through the murk and mist and gloam
To our quiet, cozy home,
Where to singing, sweet and low,
Rocks a cradle to and fro;
Where the clock's dull monotone
Telleth of the day that's done;
Where the moonbeams hover o'er
Playthings sleeping on the floor —
Where my weary wee one lies
Cometh Lady Button-Eyes.

Cometh like a fleeting ghost
From some distant eerie coast;
Never footfall can you hear

As that spirit fareth near —
Never whisper, never word
From that shadow-queen is heard.
In ethereal raiment dight,
From the realm of fay and sprite
In the depth of yonder skies
Cometh Lady Button-Eyes.

Layeth she her hands upon
My dear weary little one,
And those white hands overspread
Like a veil the curly head,
Seem to fondle and caress
Every little silken tress;
Then she smooths the eyelids down
Over those two eyes of brown —
In such soothing, tender wise
Cometh Lady Button-Eyes.

Dearest, feel upon your brow
That caressing magic now;
For the crickets in the glen
Chirp and chirp and chirp again,
While upon the haunted green
Fairies dance around their queen,
And the moonbeams hover o'er
Playthings sleeping on the floor —
Hush, my sweet! from yonder skies
Cometh Lady Button-Eyes!

10. The Ride to Bumpville

Play that my knee was a calico mare
Saddled and bridled for Bumpville;
Leap to the back of this steed if you dare,
    And gallop away to Bumpville!
I hope you'll be sure to sit fast in your seat,
For this calico mare is prodigiously fleet,
And many adventures you're likely to meet
    As you journey along to Bumpville.

This calico mare both gallops and trots
    While whisking you off to Bumpville;
She paces, she shies, and she stumbles, in spots,
    In the tortuous road to Bumpville;
And sometimes this strangely mercurial steed
Will suddenly stop and refuse to proceed,
Which, all will admit, is vexatious indeed,
    When one is *en route* to Bumpville!

She's scared of the cars when the engine goes "Toot!"
Down by the crossing at Bumpville;
You'd better look out for that treacherous brute
    Bearing you off to Bumpville!
With a snort she rears up on her hindermost heels,
And executes jigs and Virginia reels —
Words fail to explain how embarrassed one feels
    Dancing so wildly to Bumpville!

It's bumpytybump and it's jiggityjog,
    Journeying on to Bumpville;
It's over the hilltop and down through the bog
    You ride on your way to Bumpville;

It's rattletybang over boulder and stump,
There are rivers to ford, there are fences to jump,
And the corduroy road it goes bumpytybump,
    Mile after mile to Bumpville!

Perhaps you'll observe it's no easy thing
    Making the journey to Bumpville,
So I think, on the whole, it were prudent to bring
    An end to this ride to Bumpville;
For, though she has uttered no protest or plaint,
The calico mare must be blowing and faint —
What's more to the point, I'm blowed if I ain't!
    So play we have got to Bumpville!

11. Shuffle Shoon and Amber Locks

Shuffle-Shoon and Amber-Locks
    Sit together, building blocks;
Shuffle-Shoon is old and grey,
    Amber-Locks a little child,
But together at their play
    Age and Youth are reconciled,
And with sympathetic glee
Build their castles fair to see.

"When I grow to be a man"
    (So the wee one's prattle ran),
"I shall build a castle so —
    With a gateway broad and grand;
Here a pretty vine shall grow,
    There a soldier guard shall stand;
And the tower shall be so high,
Folks will wonder, by-and-by!"

Shuffle-Shoon quoth: "Yes, I know;
    Thus I builded long ago!
Here a gate and there a wall,
    Here a window, there a door;
Here a steeple wondrous tall
    Riseth ever more and more!
But the years have levelled low
What I builded long ago!"

So they gossip at their play,
    Heedless of the fleeting day;
One speaks of the Long Ago
    Where his dead hopes buried lie;
One with chubby cheeks aglow
    Prattleth of the By-and-By;
Side by side, they build their blocks
Shuffle-Shoon and Amber-Locks.

12. The Shut-Eye Train

Come, my little one, with me!
There are wondrous sights to see
    As the evening shadows fall;
    In your pretty cap and gown,
        Don't detain
        The Shut-Eye train
    "Ting-a-ling!" the bell it goeth,
    "Toot-toot!" the whistle bloweth,
And we hear the warning call:
"All aboard for Shut-Eye Town!"

Over hill and over plain
Soon will speed the Shut-Eye train!
    Through the blue where bloom the stars
    And the Mother Moon looks down
        We'll away
        To land of Fay
    Oh, the sights that we shall see there!
    Come, my little one, with me there —
'Tis a goodly train of cars
All aboard for Shut-Eye Town!

Swifter than a wild bird's flight,
Through the realms of fleecy light
    We shall speed and speed away!
    Let the Night in envy frown —
        What care we
        How wroth she be!
    To the Balow-land above us,
    To the Balow-folk who love us,
Let us hasten while we may —
All aboard for Shut-Eye Town!

Shut-Eye Town is passing fair
Golden dreams await us there;
    We shall dream those dreams, my dear,
    Till the Mother Moon goes down
        See unfold
        Delights untold!
    And in those mysterious places
    We shall see beloved faces
And beloved voices hear
In the grace of Shut-Eye Town.

Heavy are your eyes, my sweet,
Weary are your little feet
    Nestle closer up to me
    In your pretty cap and gown;
        Don't detain
        The Shut-Eye train!
    "Ting-a-ling!" the bell it goeth,
    "Toot-toot!" the whistle bloweth;
Oh, the sights that we shall see!
All aboard for Shut-Eye Town!

13. Little Oh-Dear

See, what a wonderful garden is here,
Planted and trimmed for my Little Oh-Dear!
Posies so gaudy and grass of such brown —
Search ye the country and hunt ye the town
And never ye'll meet with a garden so queer
As this one I've made for my Little Oh-Dear!

Marigolds white and buttercups blue,
Lilies all dabbled with honey and dew,
The cactus that trails over trellis and wall,
Roses and pansies and violets —all
Make proper obeisance and reverent cheer
When into her garden steps Little Oh-Dear!

And up at the top of that lavender-tree
A silver-bird singeth as only can she;
For, ever and only, she singeth the song
"I love you —I love you!" the happy day long; —
Then the echo —-the echo that smiteth me here!
"I love you, I love you," my Little Oh-Dear!

The garden may wither, the silver-bird fly —
But what careth my little precious, or I?
From her pathway of flowers that in spring-time upstart
She walketh the tenderer way in my heart;
And, oh, it is always the summer-time *here*
With that song of "I love you," my Little Oh-Dear!

14. The Fly-Away Horse

Oh, a wonderful horse is the Fly-Away Horse —
    Perhaps you have seen him before;
Perhaps, while you slept, his shadow has swept
    Through the moonlight that floats on the floor.
For it's only at night, when the stars twinkle bright,
    That the Fly-Away Horse, with a neigh
And a pull at his rein and a toss of his mane,
    Is up on his heels and away!
        The Moon in the sky,
        As he gallopeth by,
    Cries: "Oh! what a marvellous sight!"
        And the Stars in dismay
        Hide their faces away
    In the lap of old Grandmother Night.
It is yonder, out yonder, the Fly-Away Horse
    Speedeth ever and ever away —
Over meadows and lanes, over mountains and plains,
    Over streamlets that sing at their play;
And over the sea like a ghost sweepeth he,
    While the ships they go sailing below,
And he speedeth so fast that the men at the mast
    Adjudge him some portent of woe.
        "What ho there!" they cry,

Eugene Field

  As he flourishes by
With a whisk of his beautiful tail;
  And the fish in the sea
  Are as scared as can be,
From the nautilus up to the whale!
And the Fly-Away Horse seeks those far-away lands
  You little folk dream of at night —
Where candy-trees grow, and honey-brooks flow,
  And corn-fields with popcorn are white;
And the beasts in the wood are ever so good
  To children who visit them there
What glory astride of a lion to ride,
  Or to wrestle around with a bear!
    The monkeys, they say:
    "Come on, let us play,"
  And they frisk in the cocoa-nut trees:
    While the parrots, that cling
    To the peanut-vines, sing
  Or converse with comparative ease!
Off! scamper to bed--you shall ride him tonight!
  For, as soon as you've fallen asleep,
With a jubilant neigh he shall bear you away
  Over forest and hillside and deep!
But tell us, my dear, all you see and you hear
  In those beautiful lands over there,
Where the Fly-Away Horse wings his far-away course
  With the wee one consigned to his care.
    Then Grandma will cry
    In amazement: "Oh, my!"
And she'll think it could never be so;
    And only we two
    Shall know it is true —
  You and I, little precious! shall know!

15. Fiddle-Dee-Dee

To put a quietus on something means to take it out of action.

There once was a bird that lived up in a tree,
And all he could whistle was "Fiddle-dee-dee" —
A very provoking, unmusical song
For one to be whistling the summer day long!
Yet always contented and busy was he
With that vocal recurrence of "Fiddle-dee-dee."

Hard by lived a brave little soldier of four,
That weird iteration repented him sore;
"I prithee, Dear-Mother-Mine! fetch me my gun,
For, by our St. Didy! the deed must be done
That shall presently rid all creation and me
Of that ominous bird and his 'Fiddle-dee-dee'!"

Then out came Dear-Mother-Mine, bringing her son
His awfully truculent little red gun;
The stock was of pine and the barrel of tin,
The "bang" it came out where the bullet went in —
From the right kind of weapon I think you'll agree
For slaying all fowl that go "Fiddle-dee-dee!"

The brave little soldier quoth never a word,
But he up and he drew a straight bead on that bird;
And, while that vain creature provokingly sang,
The gun it went off with a terrible bang!
Then loud laughed the youth —"By my Bottle," cried he,
"I've put a quietus on 'Fiddle-dee-dee'!"

The "bang" it came out where the bullet went in

Right well have you wrought with your little gun!
Out came then Mother-Dear-Mine, saying —"My son,
Hereafter no evil at all need I fear,
With such a brave soldier as You-My-Love here!"
She kissed the dear boy. [The bird in the tree
Continued to whistle his "Fiddle-dee-dee"!]

16. The Sugar Plum Tree

Have you ever heard of the Sugar-Plum Tree?
    'Tis a marvel of great renown!
It blooms on the shore of the Lollipop sea
    In the garden of Shut-Eye Town;
The fruit that it bears is so wondrously sweet
    (As those who have tasted it say)
That good little children have only to eat
    Of that fruit to be happy next day.

When you've got to the tree, you would have a hard time
    To capture the fruit which I sing;
The tree is so tall that no person could climb
    To the boughs where the sugar-plums swing!
But up in that tree sits a chocolate cat,
    And a gingerbread dog prowls below —
And this is the way you contrive to get at
    Those sugar-plums tempting you so:

You say but the word to that gingerbread dog
    And he barks with such terrible zest
That the chocolate cat is at once all agog,
    As her swelling proportions attest.
And the chocolate cat goes cavorting around
    From this leafy limb unto that,

And the sugar-plums tumble, of course, to the ground —
    Hurrah for that chocolate cat!

There are marshmallows, gumdrops, and peppermint canes,
    With stripings of scarlet or gold,
And you carry away of the treasure that rains
    As much as your apron can hold!
So come, little child, cuddle closer to me
    In your dainty white nightcap and gown,
And I'll rock you away to that Sugar-Plum Tree
    In the garden of Shut-Eye Town.

17. Krinken

Krinken was a little child, —
It was summer when he smiled,
Oft the hoary sea and grim
Stretched its white arms out to him;
Calling, "Sun-child, come to me;
Let me warm my heart with thee!"
But the child heard not the sea.

Krinken on the beach one day
Saw a maiden Nis at play;
Frail, and very fair, was she,
Just a little child was he.
"Krinken," said the maiden Nis,
"Let me have a little kiss, —
Just a kiss, and go with me
To the summer-lands that be
Down within the silver sea."

Eugene Field

Krinken was a little child,
By the maiden Nis beguiled;
Down into the calling sea
With the maiden Nis went he.

But the sea calls out no more;
It is winter on the shore, —
Winter where that little child
Made sweet summer when he smiled;
Though 'tis summer on the sea
Where with maiden Nis went he, —
Summer, summer evermore, —
It is winter on the shore,
Winter, winter evermore.

Of the summer on the deep
Come sweet visions in my sleep;
His fair face lifts from the sea,
His dear voice calls out to me, —
These my dreams of summer be.

Krinken was a little child,
By the maiden Nis beguiled;
Oft the hoary sea and grim
Reached its longing arms to him,
Crying, "Sun-child, come to me;
Let me warm my heart with thee!"
But the sea calls out no more;
It is winter on the shore, —
Winter, cold and dark and wild;
Krinken was a little child, —
It was summer when he smiled;
Down he went into the sea,

And the winter bides with me.
Just a little child was he.

18. Pittypat and Tippytoe

"Internecine" means conflict within a group. (How amusing it is to have such a big word in a poem called "Pittypat and Tippytoe!") —A.W.

All day long they come and go —
Pittypat and Tippytoe;
    Footprints up and down the hall,
        Playthings scattered on the floor,
    Finger-marks along the wall,
        Tell-tale smudges on the door!
By these presents you shall know
Pittypat and Tippytoe.

How they riot at their play!
And a dozen times a day
    In they troop, demanding bread —
        Only buttered bread will do,
    And the butter must be spread
        Inches thick with sugar too!
And I never can say "No,
Pittypat and Tippytoe!"

Sometimes there are griefs to soothe,
Sometimes ruffled brows to smooth;
    For (I much regret to say)
        Tippytoe and Pittypat
    Sometimes interrupt their play
        With an internecine spat;

Eugene Field

Fie, for shame! to quarrel so —
Pittypat and Tippytoe!

Oh the thousand worrying things
Every day recurrent brings!
    Hands to scrub and hair to brush,
        Search for playthings gone amiss,
    Many a wee complaint to hush,
        Many a little bump to kiss;
Life seems one vain, fleeting show
To Pittypat and Tippytoe!

And when day is at an end,
There are little duds to mend:
    Little frocks are strangely torn,
        Little shoes great holes reveal,
    Little hose, but one day worn,
        Rudely yawn at toe and heel!
Who but *you* could work such woe,
Pittypat and Tippytoe?

On the floor and down the hall,
Rudely smutched upon the wall,
    There are proofs in every kind
        Of the havoc they have wrought,
    And upon my heart you'd find
        Just such trade-marks, if you sought;
Oh, how glad I am 'tis so,
Pittypat and Tippytoe!

19. So, So, Rock-a-By, So

So, so, rock-a-by so!
Off to the garden where dreamikins grow;
And here is a kiss on your winkyblink eyes,
    And here is a kiss on your dimpledown cheek
And here is a kiss for the treasure that lies
In the beautiful garden way up in the skies
    Which you seek.
Now mind these three kisses wherever you go —
So, so, rock-a-by so!

There's one little fumfay who lives there, I know,
For he dances all night where the dreamikins grow;
I send him this kiss on your droopydrop eyes,
    I send him this kiss on your rosy-red cheek.
And here is a kiss for the dream that shall rise
When the fumfay shall dance in those far-away skies
    Which you seek.
Be sure that you pay those three kisses you owe —
So, so, rock-a-by so!

And, by-low, as you rock-a-by go,
Don't forget mother who loveth you so!
And here is her kiss on your weepydeep eyes,
    And here is her kiss on your peachypink cheek,
And here is her kiss for the dreamland that lies
Like a babe on the breast of those far-away skies
    Which you seek —
The blinkywink garden where dreamikins grow —
So, so, rock-a-by so!

20. Teeny-Weeny

Every evening, after tea,
Teeny-Weeny comes to me.
And, astride my willing knee,
    Plies his lash and rides away;
Though that palfrey, all too spare,
Finds his burden hard to bear,
Teeny-Weeny doesn't care;
    He commands, and I obey!

First it's trot, and gallop, then;
Now it's back to trot again;
Teeny-Weeny likes it when
    He is riding fierce and fast.
Then his dark eyes brighter grow
And his cheeks are all aglow:
"More!" he cries, and never "Whoa!"
    Till the horse breaks down at last.

Oh, the strange and lovely sights
Teeny-Weeny sees of nights,
As he makes those famous flights
    On that wondrous horse of his!
Oftentimes before he knows,
Wearylike his eyelids close,
And, still smiling, off he goes
    Where the land of By-low is.

There he sees the folk of fay
Hard at ring-a-rosie play,
And he hears those fairies say:
    "Come, let's chase him to and fro!"

But, with a defiant shout,
Teeny puts that host to rout;
Of this tale I make no doubt,
    Every night he tells it so.

So I feel a tender pride
In my boy who dares to ride
That fierce horse of his astride,
    Off into those misty lands;
And as on my breast he lies,
Dreaming in that wondrous wise,
I caress his folded eyes,
    Pat his little dimpled hands.

On a time he went away,
Just a little while to stay,
And I'm not ashamed to say
    I was very lonely then;
Life without him was so sad,
You can fancy I was glad
And made merry when I had
    Teeny-Weeny back again!

So of evenings, after tea,
When he toddles up to me
And goes tugging at my knee,
    You should hear his palfrey neigh!
You should see him prance and shy,
When, with an exulting cry,
Teeny-Weeny, vaulting high,
    Plies his lash and rides away!

21. Buttercup, Poppy, Forget-me-not

Buttercup, Poppy, Forget-me-not —
These three bloomed in a garden spot;
And once, all merry with song and play,
A little one heard three voices say:
    "Shine and shadow, summer and spring,
      O thou child with the tangled hair
   And laughing eyes! we three shall bring
      Each an offering passing fair."
The little one did not understand,
But they bent and kissed the dimpled hand.

Buttercup gamboled all day long,
Sharing the little one's mirth and song;
Then, stealing along on misty gleams,
Poppy came bearing the sweetest dreams.
    Playing and dreaming — and that was all
      Till once a sleeper would not awake;
   Kissing the little face under the pall,
      We thought of the words the third flower spake;
And we found betimes in a hallowed spot
The solace and peace of Forget-me-not.

Buttercup shareth the joy of day,
Glinting with gold the hours of play;
Bringeth the poppy sweet repose,
When the hands would fold and the eyes would close;
   And after it all — the play and the sleep
     Of a little life — what cometh then?
   To the hearts that ache and the eyes that weep
     A new flower bringeth God's peace again.

Each one serveth its tender lot —
Buttercup, Poppy, Forget-me-not.

22. Wynken, Blynken, and Nod

Wynken, Blynken, and Nod one night
    Sailed off in a wooden shoe —
Sailed on a river of crystal light,
    Into a sea of dew.
"Where are you going, and what do you wish?"
    The old moon asked the three.
"We have come to fish for the herring fish
    That live in this beautiful sea;
Nets of silver and gold have we!"
        Said Wynken,
        Blynken,
        And Nod.

The old moon laughed and sang a song,
    As they rocked in the wooden shoe,
And the wind that sped them all night long
    Ruffled the waves of dew.
The little stars were the herring fish
    That lived in that beautiful sea —
"Now cast your nets wherever you wish —
    Never afeard are we";
So cried the stars to the fishermen three:
        Wynken,
        Blynken,
        And Nod.

All night long their nets they threw

To the stars in the twinkling foam —
Then down from the skies came the wooden shoe
   Bringing the fishermen home;
'Twas all so pretty a sail it seemed
   As if it could not be,
And some folks thought 'twas a dreamed they'd dreamed
   Of sailing that beautiful sea —
But I shall name you the fishermen three:
      Wynken,
      Blynken,
      And Nod.

Wynken and Blynken are two little eyes,
   And Nod is a little head,
And the wooden shoe that sailed the skies
   Is a wee one's trundle-bed.
So shut your eyes while mother sings
   Of wonderful sights that be,
And you shall see the beautiful things
   As you rock in the misty sea,
Where the old shoe rocked the fishermen three:
      Wynken,
      Blynken,
      And Nod.

23. Little Mistress Sans-Merci

The English poet John Keats wrote a famous poem called "La Belle Dame sans Merci," or "The Beautiful Lady Without Mercy." It is about a knight who meets "a lady in the meads, Full beautiful—a faery's child"; but, as in many fairy tales, this lady turns out to be dangerous. Field is having a bit of fun with Keats' title, by saying that this tiny girl commands his life in just such a way. "Sans-Merci" is usually pronounced something close to "Sahns Mare See."—A.W.

Little Mistress Sans-Merci
Fareth world-wide, fancy free:
    Trotteth cooing to and fro,
        And her cooing is command —
    Never ruled there yet, I trow,
        Mightier despot in the land.
And my heart it lieth where
Mistress Sans-Merci doth fare.

Little Mistress Sans-Merci —
She hath made a slave of me!
    "Go," she biddeth, and I go —
        "Come," and I am fain to come —
    Never mercy doth she show,
        Be she wroth or frolicsome,
Yet am I content to be
Slave to Mistress Sans-Merci!

Little Mistress Sans-Merci
Hath become so dear to me
    That I count as passing sweet
        All the pain her moods impart,
    And I bless the little feet
        That go trampling on my heart:

Ah, how lonely life would be
But for little Sans-Merci!

Little Mistress Sans-Merci,
Cuddle close this night to me,
    And the heart, which all day long
        Ruthless thou hast trod upon,
    Shall outpour a soothing song
        For its best belovèd one —
All its tenderness for thee,
Little Mistress Sans-Merci!

24. Hi-Spy

Strange that the city thoroughfare,
    Noisy and bustling all the day,
Should with the night renounce its care
    And lend itself to children's play!

Oh, girls are girls, and boys are boys,
    And have been so since Abel's birth,
And shall be so till dolls and toys
    Are with the children swept from earth.

The self-same sport that crowns the clay
    Of many a Syrian shepherd's son,
Beguiles the little lads at play
    By night in stately Babylon.

I hear their voices in the street,
    Yet 'tis so different now from then!
Come, brother! from your winding-sheet,
    And let us two be boys again!

25. Little Boy Blue

The little toy dog is covered with dust,
    But sturdy and staunch he stands;
And the little toy soldier is red with rust,
    And the musket moulds in his hands.
Time was when the little toy dog was new,
    And the soldier was passing fair;
And that was the time when our Little Boy Blue
    Kissed them and put them there.

"Now, don't you go till I come," he said,
    "And don't you make any noise!"
So, toddling off to his trundle-bed,
    He dreamt of the pretty toys;
And, as he was dreaming, an angel song
    Awakened our Little Boy Blue —
Oh! the years are many, the years are long,
    But the little toy friends are true!

Aye, faithful to Little Boy Blue they stand,
    Each in the same old place —
Awaiting the touch of a little hand,
    The smile of a little face;
And they wonder, as waiting the long years through
    In the dust of that little chair,
What has become of our Little Boy Blue,
    Since he kissed them and put them there.

26. Heigho, My Dearie

Moonbeam floateth from the skies,
    Whispering: "Heigho, my dearie;
I would spin a web before your eyes —
A beautiful web of silver light
Wherein is many a wondrous sight
Of a radiant garden leagues away,
Where the softly tinkling lilies sway
And the snow-white lambkins are at play —
    Heigho, my dearie!"

A brownie stealeth from the vine,
    Singing: "Heigho, my dearie;
And will you hear this song of mine —
A song of the land of murk and mist
Where bideth the bud the dew hath kist?
Then let the moonbeam's web of light
Be spun before thee silvery white,
And I shall sing the livelong night —
    Heigho, my dearie!"

The night wind speedeth from the sea,
    Murmuring: "Heigho, my dearie;
I bring a mariner's prayer for thee;
So let the moonbeam veil thine eyes,
And the brownie sing thee lullabies —
But I shall rock thee to and fro,
Kissing the brow *he* loveth so.
And the prayer shall guard thy bed, I trow —
    Heigho, my dearie!"

27. Fairy and Child

Oh, listen, little Dear-My-Soul,
    To the fairy voices calling,
For the moon is high in the misty sky
    And the honey dew is falling;
To the midnight feast in the clover bloom
    The bluebells are a-ringing,
And it's "Come away to the land of fay"
    That the katydid is singing.

Oh, slumber, little Dear-My-Soul,
    And hand in hand we'll wander —
Hand in hand to the beautiful land
    Of Balow, away off yonder;
Or we'll sail along in a lily leaf
    Into the white moon's halo —
Over a stream of mist and dream
    Into the land of Balow.

Or, you shall have two beautiful wings —
    Two gossamer wings and airy,
And all the while shall the old moon smile
    And think you a little fairy;
And you shall dance in the velvet sky,
    And the silvery stars shall twinkle
And dream sweet dreams as over their beams
    Your footfalls softly tinkle.

28. Child and Mother

O Mother-my-love, if you'll give me your hand,
    And go where I ask you to wander,

I will lead you away to a beautiful land —
    The Dreamland that's waiting out yonder.
We'll walk in a sweet-posie garden out there
    Where moonlight and starlight are streaming
And the flowers and the birds are filling the air
    With the fragrance and music of dreaming.

There'll be no little tired-out boy to undress,
    No questions or cares to perplex you;
There'll be no little bruises or bumps to caress,
    Nor patching of stockings to vex you.
For I'll rock you away on a silver-dew stream,
    And sing you asleep when you're weary,
And no one shall know of our beautiful dream
    But you and your own little dearie.

And when I am tired I'll nestle my head
    In the bosom that's soothed me so often,
And the wide-awake stars shall sing in my stead
    A song which our dreaming shall soften.
So, Mother-My-Love, let me take your dear hand,
    And away through the starlight we'll wander —
Away through the mist to the beautiful land —
    The Dreamland that's waiting out yonder!

29. Ganderfeather's Gift

"Attenuate" means weak or thin, and "buxom," as it is used here, is the opposite: plump and lively. A "sprite" is an elf or a fairy.

I was just a little thing
    When a fairy came and kissed me;
Floating in upon the light
Of a haunted summer night,

Lo, the fairies came to sing
Pretty slumber songs and bring
    Certain boons that else had missed me.
From a dream I turned to see
What those strangers brought for me,
    When that fairy up and kissed me —
    Here, upon this cheek, he kissed me!

Simmerdew was there, but she
    Did not like me altogether;
Daisybright and Turtledove,
Pilfercurds and Honeylove,
Thistleblow and Amberglee
On that gleaming, ghostly sea
    Floated from the misty heather,
And around my trundle-bed
Frisked, and looked, and whispering said —
    Solemnlike and all together:
    "*You* shall kiss him, Ganderfeather!"

Ganderfeather kissed me then —
    Ganderfeather, quaint and merry!
No attenuate sprite was he,
——But as buxom as could be; —
Kissed me twice, and once again,
And the others shouted when
    On my cheek uprose a berry
Somewhat like a mole, mayhap,
But the kiss-mark of that chap
    Ganderfeather, passing merry —
    Humorsome, but kindly, very!

I was just a tiny thing

When the prankish Ganderfeather
Brought this curious gift to me
With his fairy kisses three;
Yet with honest pride I sing
That same gift he chose to bring
    Out of yonder haunted heather.
Other charms and friendships fly —
Constant friends this mole and I,
    Who have been so long together.
    Thank you, little Ganderfeather!

30. Telling the Bees

A folk custom in many European countries and the U.S. is that it's important to tell the bees about any significant family events. It's especially important to tell the bees whenever a member of the household dies. If they are not told, they might leave the hive, or possibly even worse luck will befall the household. —W.C.

Out of the house where the slumberer lay
Grandfather came one summer day,
And under the pleasant orchard trees
He spake this wise to the murmuring bees:
    "The clover-bloom that kissed her feet
    And the posie-bed where she used to play,
    Have honey store, but none so sweet
    As ere our little one went away.
    O bees, sing soft, and, bees, sing low;
    For she is gone who loved you so."

A wonder fell on the listening bees
Under those pleasant orchard trees,
And in their toil that summer day
Ever their murmuring seemed to say:
    "Child, O child, the grass is cool,

And the posies are waking to hear the song
Of the bird that swings by the shaded pool,
Waiting for one that tarrieth long."
'Twas so they called to the little one then,
As if to call her back again.

O gentle bees, I have come to say
That grandfather fell asleep to-day,
And we know by the smile on grandfather's face
He has found his dear one's biding-place.
So, bees, sing soft, and, bees, sing low,
As over the honey-fields you sweep
To the trees abloom and the flowers ablow
Sing of grandfather fast asleep;
And ever beneath these orchard trees
Find cheer and shelter, gentle bees.

31. Contentment

"Foliage of vermilion hue" means red feathers.

Once on a time an old red hen
    Went strutting round with pompous clucks,
For she had little babies ten,
    A part of which were tiny ducks.
"'Tis very rare that hens," said she,
    "Have baby ducks as well as chicks —
But I possess, as you can see,
    Of chickens four and ducklings six!"

A season later, this old hen
    Appeared, still cackling of her luck,
For, though she boasted babies ten,
    Not one among them was a duck!

Eugene Field

"'Tis well," she murmured, brooding o'er
    The little chicks of fleecy down —
"My babies now will stay ashore,
    And, consequently, cannot drown!"

The following spring the old red hen
Clucked just as proudly as of yore —
But lo! her babes were ducklings ten,
Instead of chickens, as before!
"'Tis better," said the old red hen,
As she surveyed her waddling brood;
"A little water now and then
Will surely do my darlings good!"

But, oh! alas, how very sad!
    When gentle spring rolled round again.
The eggs eventuated bad,
    And childless was the old red hen!
Yet patiently she bore her woe,
    And still she wore a cheerful air,
And said: "'Tis best these things are so
    For babies are a dreadful care!"

I half suspect that many men,
    And many, many women, too,
Could learn a lesson from the hen
    With foliage of vermilion hue.
She ne'er presumed to take offence
    At any fate that might befall,
But meekly bowed to Providence.
    She was contented —that was all!

More poems by Eugene Field

32. The Naughty Doll

My dolly is a dreadful care, —
 Her name is Miss Amandy;
I dress her up and curl her hair,
 And feed her taffy candy.
Yet heedless of the pleading voice
 Of her devoted mother,
She will not wed her mother's choice,
 But says she'll wed another.

I'd have her wed the china vase, —
 There is no Dresden rarer;
You might go searching every place
 And never find a fairer.
He is a gentle, pinkish youth, —
 Of that there's no denying;
Yet when I think of him forsooth,
 Amandy falls to crying!

She loves the drum–that's very plain —
 And scorns the case so clever;
And weeping, vows she will remain
 A spinster doll forever!
The protestations of the drum
 I am convinced are hollow;
When once distressing times should come,
 How soon would ruin follow!

Yet all in vain the Dresden boy
 From yonder mantel woos her;

A mania for that vulgar toy,
    The noisy drum, imbues her!
In vain I wheel her to and fro,
    And reason with her mildly, —
Her waxen tears in torrents flow,
    Her sawdust heart beats wildly.

I'm sure that when I'm big and tall,
    And wear long trailing dresses,
I sha'n't encourage beaux at all
    Till mama acquiesces;
Our choice will be a suitor then
    As pretty as this vase is, —
Oh, how we'll hate the noisy men
    With whiskers on their faces!

33. Over the Hills and Far Away

Over the hills and far away,
A little boy steals from his morning play,
And under the blossoming apple-tree
He lies and dreams of the things to be:
Of battles fought and of victories won,
Of wrongs o'erthrown and of great deeds done —
Of the valor that he shall prove some day,
Over the hills and far away —
    Over the hills and far away!

Over the hills and far away
It's, oh, for the toil of the livelong day!
But it mattereth not to the soul aflame
With a love for riches and power and fame!
On, O man! while the sun is high —

On to the certain joys that lie
Yonder where blazeth the noon of day.
Over the hills and far away —
    Over the hills and far away!

Over the hills and far away
An old man lingers at close of day;
Now that his journey is almost done,
His battles fought and his victories won —
The old-time honesty and truth,
The trustfulness and the friends of youth,
Home and mother —where are they?
Over the hills and far away —
    Over the years and far away!

34. Inscription for My Little Son's Silver Plate

When thou dost eat from off this plate,
I charge thee be thou temperate;
Unto thine elders at the board
Do thou sweet reverence accord;
And, though to dignity inclined,
Unto the serving-folk be kind;
Be ever mindful of the poor,
Nor turn them hungry from the door;
And unto God, for health and food
And all that in thy life is good,
Give thou thy heart in gratitude.

35. In the Firelight

The fire upon the hearth is low,
    And there is stillness everywhere,
    And, like wing'd spirits, here and there
The firelight shadows fluttering go.
And as the shadows round me creep,
    A childish treble breaks the gloom,
    And softly from a further room
Comes: "Now I lay me down to sleep."

And, somehow with that little pray'r
    And that sweet treble in my ears,
    My thought goes back to distant years,
And lingers with a dear one there;
And as I hear my child's amen,
    My mother's faith comes back to me —
    Crouched at her side I seem to be,
And mother holds my hands again.

Oh, for an hour in that dear place —
    Oh, for that childish trust sublime —
    Oh, for a glimpse of mother's face!
Yet, as the shadows round me creep,
    I do not seem to be alone —
    Sweet magic of that treble tone
And "Now I lay me down to sleep!"

36. *from* Jest 'Fore Christmas

"No flies on me" is an expression meaning alert and clever. It is said to have originated in Australia in the 1840's.

"Chawnk" is a dialect word used in Vermont (where Field spent his childhood). It means "chew."

Father calls me William, sister calls me Will,
Mother calls me Willie, but the fellers call me Bill!
Mighty glad I ain't a girl —ruther be a boy,
Without them sashes, curls, an' things that's worn by Fauntleroy!
Love to chawnk green apples an' go swimmin' in the lake —
Hate to take the castor-ile they give for belly-ache!
'Most all the time, the whole year round, there ain't no flies on me,
But jest 'fore Christmas I'm as good as I kin be!

Got a yeller dog named Sport, sick him on the cat;
First thing she knows she doesn't know where she is at!
Got a clipper sled, an' when us kids goes out to slide,
'Long comes the grocery cart, an' we all hook a ride!
But sometimes when the grocery man is worrited an' cross,
He reaches at us with his whip, an' larrups up his hoss,
An' then I laff an' holler, "Oh, ye never teched *me!*"
But jest 'fore Christmas I'm as good as I kin be!

And then old Sport he hangs around, so solemn-like an' still,
His eyes they seem a-sayin': "What's the matter, little Bill?"
The old cat sneaks down off her perch an' wonders what's become
Of them two enemies of hern that used to make things hum!
But I am so perlite an' tend so earnestly to biz,
That mother says to father: "How improved our Willie is!"
But father, havin' been a boy hisself, suspicions me
When, jest 'fore Christmas, I'm as good as I kin be!

For Christmas, with its lots an' lots of candies, cakes an' toys,
Was made, they say, for proper kids an' not for naughty boys;
So wash yer face an' bresh yer hair, an' mind yer p's and q's,
And don't bust out yer pantaloons, and don't wear out yer shoes;
Say "Yessum" to the ladies, an' "Yessur" to the men,
An' when they's company, don't pass yer plate for pie again;
But, thinkin' of the things yer'd like to see upon that tree,
Jest 'fore Christmas be as good as yer kin be!

37. Little Homer's Slate

After dear old grandma died,
    Hunting through an oaken chest
In the attic, we espied
    What repaid our childish quest;
'Twas a homely little slate,
Seemingly of ancient date.

On its quaint and battered face
    Was the picture of a cart,
Drawn with all that awkward grace
    Which betokens childish art;
But what meant this legend, pray:
"Homer drew this yesterday"?

Mother recollected then
    What the years were fain to hide —
She was but a baby when
    Little Homer lived and died;
Forty years, so mother said,
Little Homer had been dead.

This one secret through those years
    Grandma kept from all apart,
Hallowed by her lonely tears
    And the breaking of her heart;
While each year that sped away
Seemed to her but yesterday.

So the homely little slate
    Grandma's baby's fingers pressed,
To a memory consecrate,
    Lieth in the oaken chest,
Where, unwilling we should know,
Grandma put it, years ago.

38. The Hawthorne Children

The Hawthorne children —seven in all—
    Are famous friends of mine,
And with what pleasure I recall
How, years ago, one gloomy fall,
    I took a tedious railway line
And journeyed by slow stages down
Unto that sleepy seaport town
    (Albeit one worth seeing),
        Were Hildegarde, John, Henry, Fred,
And Beatrix and Gwendolen
And she that was the baby then —
    These famous seven, as aforesaid,
        Lived, moved, and had their being.

The Hawthorne children gave me such
    A welcome by the sea,

Eugene Field

That the eight of us were soon in touch,
And though their mother marveled much,
 Happy as larks were we!
Egad I was a boy again
With Henry, John, and Gwendolen!
 And, oh! the funny capers
  I cut with Hildegarde and Fred!
The pranks we heedless children played,
The deafening, awful noise we made —
 'Twould shock my family, if they read
  About it in the papers!

The Hawthorne children all were smart;
 The girls, as I recall,
Had comprehended every art
Appealing to the head and heart,
 The boys were gifted, all;
'Twas Hildegard that showed me how
To hitch the horse and milk a cow
 And cook the best of suppers;
 With Beatrix upon the sands
I sprinted daily, and was beat,
While Henry stumped me to the feat
 Of walking round upon my hands
  Instead of on my "uppers."

The Hawthorne children liked me best
 Of evenings, after tea;
For then, by general request,
I spun them yarns about the west —
 And *all* involving Me!
I represented how I'd slain
The bison on the gore-smeared plain,

And divers tales of wonder
>	I'd told of how I'd fought and bled
In Injun scrimages galore,
Til Mrs. Hawthorne quoth, "No more!"
>	And packed her darlings off to bed
>	>	To dream of blood and thunder!

They must have changed a deal since then:
>	The misses tall and fair,
And those three lusty, handsome men,
Would they be girls and boys again
>	Were I to happen there,
Down in that spot beside the sea
Where we had such tumultuous glee
>	In dull autumnal weather?
>	>	Ah me! the years go swiftly by,
And yet how fondly I recall
The week when we were children all —
>	Dear Hawthorne children, you and I —
>	>	Just eight of us, together!

39. The Death of Robin Hood

"Mickle" means a great amount.

"Give me my bow," said Robin Hood,
>	"An arrow give to me;
And where 't is shot mark thou that spot,
>	For there my grave shall be."

Then Little John did make no sign,
>	And not a word he spake;
But he smiled, altho' with mickle woe
>	His heart was like to break.

Eugene Field

He raised his master in his arms,
  And set him on his knee;
And Robin's eyes beheld the skies,
  The shaws, the greenwood tree.

The brook was babbling as of old,
  The birds sang full and clear,
And the wild-flowers gay like a carpet lay
  In the path of the timid deer.

"O Little John," said Robin Hood,
  "Meseemeth now to be
Standing with you so stanch and true
  Under the greenwood tree.

"And all around I hear the sound
  Of Sherwood long ago,
And my merry men come back again, —
  You know, sweet friend, you know!

"Now mark this arrow; where it falls,
  When I am dead dig deep,
And bury me there in the greenwood where
  I would forever sleep."

He twanged his bow. Upon its course
  The clothyard arrow sped,
And when it fell in yonder dell,
  Brave Robin Hood was dead.

The sheriff sleeps in a marble vault,
  The king in a shroud of gold;

And upon the air with a chanted pray'r
  Mingles the mock of mould.

But the deer draw to the shady pool,
  The birds sing blithe and free,
And the wild-flow'rs bloom o'er a hidden tomb
  Under the greenwood tree.

James Whitcomb Riley (1849-1916)
Biographical Sketch by Wendi Capehart

James Whitcomb Riley is known as "The Hoosier Poet," because he is from the state of Indiana, and Indiana is the Hoosier State. Nobody knows for sure what Hoosier meant, although there are many guesses. One is that in the frontier days, it was customary to stand outside the door of a cabin and shout "Who's here?" There's an Indiana accent or dialect that isn't quite southern but isn't northern either, and "who's here" does sound a little bit like "hoosier." But there are at least half a dozen other guesses, and none has more support than another. Whether that is the source of Hoosier or not, Riley certainly popularized this dialect in many of his regional poems.

Dialect poetry is poetry that attempts to reproduce a specific accent or regional style of speech. It can be very difficult to read if you are not familiar with how the dialect sounds in real life.

I once sat in a university course on children's literature where the professor said that Riley's dialect poems were making fun of the speech of freed slaves; but this could hardly be more false. Riley isn't making fun of anybody. Authentic dialect poetry is almost never mocking people, but is warmly and affectionately attempting to preserve and reproduce the real speech patterns of people the poet knows and loves. Riley's poems really do represent the way many country people spoke, and sometimes still do speak in Indiana. If the dialect in those poems gives you trouble, if it is at all possible, look for a recorded performance of some of the dialect poems, done by somebody who knows the sound of the Hoosier country accent.

Riley was born in Greenfield, Indiana. He was one of six children. His father was a lawyer who often brought interesting guests home for dinner —some famous, and some destitute and in need of help. His mother read to the children often, and fairy tales, folk tales, and ghost stories were among their favorites. This gave young James and his siblings exposure to all kinds of people.

The family moved to Indianapolis to be closer to the father's work, but they kept the family farm for food and extra income. This was fortunate, since later, after the Civil War, Mr. Riley Senior was unable to find work consistently, and the family had to return to the farm and eke out a living there.

James Whitcomb Riley was, at best, an indifferent student. He hated school and played truant often. He preferred spending his time at the old swimming hole and other haunts which would later show up in so many of his poems. For this reason, he didn't finish school until he was twenty, and even then, his last completed full grade was only the eighth grade. He had very little to say about his teachers, except for his last teacher, who encouraged him to read good books.

When he finished his school, his father wanted him to become a lawyer, but he was not well equipped for any work requiring discipline and education. His father and he argued often, and at last he left home to join a traveling medicine show as a huckster. He also made some money from painting signs for stores and taverns for a while. Eventually he settled down to writing little articles for the local paper.

Newspapers at the time often published poems, and poetry was popular then. Riley attempted to get his poems published this way. However, his poems were seldom accepted by the larger papers, so his efforts weren't paying enough to support him.

He thought his poems were really very good, but they weren't being accepted just because he wasn't already famous, so he decided to play a little trick on the editors of the papers. He wrote a poem after the style of Edgar Allan Poe, and submitted it to the paper as a newly discovered Poe poem. He expected to see his work widely accepted. That is not what happened. The first paper published the poem as a Poe discovery; but other papers either did not bother to publish it at all, or published it only to challenge its authenticity. Most scholars pointed out that it was inferior to Poe's work. This must have been a crushing blow to his ego.

He continued to write poems, improving them little by little. Meanwhile, he was struggling with both his home life and his work life. His mother died, and he blamed his father, who had come back from his service in the war a changed man, and not for the better. He and his father were estranged, and James Whitcomb Riley turned to alcohol and developed a serious drinking problem which he never overcame.

He continued to write and submit his poems. He also began performing on the public circuit, as the poet Eugene Field had. He carefully groomed his public persona, changing his dress from the more flamboyant styles he had previously preferred to more homespun appearance. He basically recreated himself as a country poet, changing his clothing and demeanor to match the fictional character he had created. His public performances were received well by the public. All poetry is best when read aloud, dialect poetry, more than other forms, is best when read aloud well. He was very popular. He began to make enough money to fully support himself in comfort, and he was even able to support two of his sisters and their children (one sister was divorced, one widowed).

His poems were often based on real people and places he had known. "The Raggedy Man" was a German hired hand who had worked for his father. "Little Orphant Annie" was a real person, an orphan girl who came to work for the family when their father left for the Civil War. Her real name was Allie, but a printer's error altered it to Annie, and Riley didn't correct it. Allie grew up, married, and lived in the area for the rest of her life, and returned to help out in the Riley home many times in her adult life.

Riley died in 1916, and though he had many personal flaws, he was a devoted brother and a doting uncle, and his poetry delighted and amused thousands of families during his lifetime, and for many years afterward.

01. When the Frost is on the Punkin

When the frost is on the punkin and the fodder's in the shock,
And you hear the kyouck and gobble of the struttin' turkey-cock,
And the clackin' of the guineys, and the cluckin' of the hens,
And the rooster's hallylooyer as he tiptoes on the fence;
O, it's then's the times a feller is a-feelin' at his best,
With the risin' sun to greet him from a night of peaceful rest,
As he leaves the house, bareheaded, and goes to feed the stock,
When the frost is on the punkin and the fodder's in the shock.

They's something kindo' harty-like about the atmusfere
When the heat of summer's over and the coolin' fall is here —
Of course we miss the flowers, and the blossums on the trees,
And the mumble of the hummin'-birds and buzzin' of the bees;
But the air's so appetizin'; and the landscape through the haze
Of a crisp and sunny morning of the airly autumn days
Is a pictur' that no painter has the colorin' to mock —
When the frost is on the punkin and the fodder's in the shock.

The husky, rusty russel of the tossels of the corn,
And the raspin' of the tangled leaves, as golden as the morn;
The stubble in the furries —kindo' lonesome-like, but still
A-preachin' sermons to us of the barns they growed to fill;
The strawsack in the medder, and the reaper in the shed;
The hosses in theyr stalls below–the clover overhead! —
O, it sets my hart a-clickin' like the tickin' of a clock,
When the frost is on the punkin, and the fodder's in the shock!

Then your apples all is gethered, and the ones a feller keeps
Is poured around the celler-floor in red and yeller heaps;
And your cider-makin's over, and your wimmern-folks is through
With their mince and apple-butter, and theyr souse and saussage, too!

I don't know how to tell it —but ef sich a thing could be
As the Angels wantin' boardin', and they'd call around on me —
I'd want to 'commodate 'em—all the whole-indurin' flock —
When the frost is on the punkin and the fodder's in the shock!

02. Little Orphant Annie

Inscribed, with All Faith and Affection:
To all the little children: —the happy ones; and sad ones;
The sober and the silent ones; the boisterous and glad ones;
The good ones —Yes, the good ones, too; and all the lovely bad ones.

Little Orphant Annie's come to our house to stay,
An' wash the cups an' saucers up, an' brush the crumbs away,
An' shoo the chickens off the porch, an' dust the hearth, an' sweep,
An' make the fire, an' bake the bread, an' earn her board-an'-keep;
An' all us other children, when the supper-things is done,
We set around the kitchen fire an' has the mostest fun
A-list'nin' to the witch-tales 'at Annie tells about,
An' the Gobble-uns 'at gits you
 Ef you
  Don't
   Watch
    Out!

Wunst they wuz a little boy wouldn't say his prayers, —
An' when he went to bed at night, away up-stairs,
His Mammy heerd him holler, an' his Daddy heerd him bawl,
An' when they turn't the kivvers down, he wuzn't there at all!
An' they seeked him in the rafter room, an' cubby-hole, an' press,
An' seeked him up the chimbly-flue, an' ever'-wheres, I guess;
But all they ever found wuz thist his pants an' roundabout: —
An' the Gobble-uns 'll git you

        Ef you
         Don't
          Watch
           Out!

An' one time a little girl 'ud allus laugh an' grin,
An' make fun of ever' one, an' all her blood-an'-kin;
An' wunst, when they was "company," an' ole folks wuz there,
She mocked 'em an' shocked 'em, an' said she didn't care!
An' thist as she kicked her heels, an' turn't to run an' hide,
They wuz two great big Black Things a-standin' by her side,
An' they snatched her through the ceilin' 'fore she knowed what she's about!
An' the Gobble-uns 'll git you
 Ef you
  Don't
   Watch
    Out!

An' little Orphant Annie says, when the blaze is blue,
An' the lamp-wick sputters, an' the wind goes woo-oo!
An' you hear the crickets quit, an' the moon is gray,
An' the lightnin'-bugs in dew is all squenched away, —
You better mind yer parunts, an' yer teachurs fond an' dear,
An' cherish them 'at loves you, an' dry the orphant's tear,
An' he'p the pore an' needy ones 'at clusters all about,
Er the Gobble-uns 'll git you
 Ef you
  Don't
   Watch
    Out!

03. The Raggedy Man

O the Raggedy Man! He works fer Pa;
An' he's the goodest man ever you saw!
He comes to our house every day,
An' waters the horses, an' feeds 'em hay;
An' he opens the shed —an' we all ist laugh
When he drives out our little old wobble-ly calf;
An' nen —ef our hired girl says he can —
He milks the cow fer 'Lizabuth Ann. —
Ain't he a' awful good Raggedy Man?
Raggedy! Raggedy! Raggedy Man!

W'y, The Raggedy Man —-he's ist so good,
He splits the kindlin' an' chops the wood;
An' nen he spades in our garden, too,
An' does most things 'at boys can't do. —
He clumbed clean up in our big tree
An' shooked a' apple down fer me —
An' 'nother 'n', too, fer 'Lizabuth Ann —
An' 'nother 'n', too, fer The Raggedy Man. —
Ain't he a' awful kind Raggedy Man?
Raggedy! Raggedy! Raggedy Man!

An' The Raggedy Man one time say he
Pick' roast' rambos from a' orchurd-tree,
An' et 'em–all ist roast' an' hot! —
An' it's so, too! —'cause a corn-crib got
Afire one time an' all burn' down
On "The Smoot Farm," 'bout four mile from town —
On "The Smoot Farm"! Yes —an' the hired han'

'At worked there nen 'uz The Raggedy Man! —
Ain't he the beatin'est Raggedy Man?
Raggedy! Raggedy! Raggedy Man!

The Raggedy Man's so good an' kind
He'll be our "horsey," an' "haw" an' mind
Ever'thing 'at you make him do —
An' won't run off — 'less you want him to!
I drived him wunst way down our lane
An' he got skeered, when it 'menced to rain,
An' ist rared up an' squealed and run
Purt' nigh away! —an' it's all in fun!
Nen he skeered ag'in at a' old tin can ...
Whoa! y' old runaway Raggedy Man!
Raggedy! Raggedy! Raggedy Man!

An' The Raggedy Man, he knows most rhymes,
An' tells 'em, ef I be good, sometimes:
Knows 'bout Giunts, an' Griffuns, an' Elves,
An' the Squidgicum-Squees 'at swallers the'rselves:
An', wite by the pump in our pasture-lot,
He showed me the hole 'at the Wunks is got,
'At lives 'way deep in the ground, an' can
Turn into me, er 'Lizabuth Ann!
Er Ma, er Pa, er The Raggedy Man!
Ain't he a funny old Raggedy Man?
Raggedy! Raggedy! Raggedy Man!

An' wunst, when The Raggedy Man come late,
An' pigs ist root' thue the garden-gate,
He 'tend like the pigs 'uz bears an' said,
"Old Bear-shooter'll shoot 'em dead!"
An' race' an' chase' 'em, an' they'd ist run

When he pint his hoe at 'em like it's a gun
An' go "Bang!–Bang!" nen 'tend he stan'
An' load up his gun ag'in! Raggedy Man!
He's an old Bear-shooter Raggedy Man!
Raggedy! Raggedy! Raggedy Man!

An' sometimes The Raggedy Man lets on
We're little prince-children, an' old King's gone
To git more money, an' lef' us there —
And Robbers is ist thick ever'where;
An' nen–ef we all won't cry, fer shore —
The Raggedy Man he'll come and "'splore
The Castul-halls," an' steal the "gold" —
An' steal us, too, an' grab an' hold
An' pack us off to his old "Cave"! —An'
Haymow's the "cave" o' The Raggedy Man! —
Raggedy! Raggedy! Raggedy Man!

The Raggedy Man–one time, when he
Wuz makin' a little bow-'n'-orry fer me,
Says "When you're big like your Pa is,
Air you go' to keep a fine store like his —
An' be a rich merchunt–an' wear fine clothes? —
Er what air you go' to be, goodness knows?"
An' nen he laughed at 'Lizabuth Ann,
An' I says "'M go' to be a Raggedy Man! —
I'm ist go' to be a nice Raggedy Man!"
Raggedy! Raggedy! Raggedy Man!

04. The Bumblebee

You better not fool with a Bumblebee! —
Ef you don't think they can sting —you'll see!
They're lazy to look at, an' kind o' go
Buzzin' an' bummin' aroun' so slow,
An' ac' so slouchy an' all fagged out,
Danglin' their legs as they drone about
The hollyhawks 'at they can't climb in
'Ithout ist a-tumble-un out ag'in!
Wunst I watched one climb clean 'way
In a jimson-blossom, I did, one day, —
An' I ist grabbed it–an' nen let go —
An' "Ooh-ooh! Honey! I told ye so!"
Says The Raggedy Man; an' he ist run
An' pullt out the stinger, an' don't laugh none,
An' says: "They has be'n folks, I guess,
'At thought I wuz predjudust, more er less, —
Yit I still muntain 'at a Bumblebee
Wears out his welcome too quick fer me!"

05. Granny

Granny's come to our house,
And ho! my lawzy-daisy!
All the childern round the place
Is ist a-runnin' crazy!
Fetched a cake fer little Jake,
And fetched a pie fer Nanny,
And fetched a pear fer all the pack
That runs to kiss their Granny!

James Whitcomb Riley

Lucy Ellen's in her lap,
And Wade and Silas Walker
Both's a-ridin' on her foot,
And 'Pollos on the rocker;
And Marthy's twins, from Aunt Marinn's,
And little Orphant Annie,
All's a-eatin' gingerbread
And giggle-un at Granny!

Tells us all the fairy tales
Ever thought er wundered —
And 'bundance o' other stories —
Bet she knows a hunderd! —
Bob's the one fer "Whittington,"
And "Golden Locks" fer Fanny!
Hear 'em laugh and clap their hands,
Listenin' at Granny!

"Jack the Giant-Killer" 's good;
And "Bean-Stalk" 's another! —
So's the one of "Cinderell'"
And her old godmother; —
That-un's best of all the rest —
Bestest one of any, —
Where the mices scampers home
Like we runs to Granny!

Granny's come to our house,
Ho! my lawzy-daisy!
All the childern round the place
Is ist a-runnin' crazy!
Fetched a cake fer little Jake,
And fetched a pie fer Nanny,

And fetched a pear fer all the pack
That runs to kiss their Granny!

06. Our Hired Girl

A "maccordeun" is Riley's dialect spelling of an accordion (a musical instrument). Parched corn is similar to popcorn.

Our hired girl, she's 'Lizabuth Ann;
An' she can cook best things to eat!
She ist puts dough in our pie-pan,
An' pours in somepin' 'at's good an' sweet;
An' nen she salts it all on top
With cinnamon; an' nen she'll stop
An' stoop an' slide it, ist as slow,
In th' old cook-stove, so's 'twon't slop
An' git all spilled; nen bakes it, so
It's custard-pie, first thing you know!
An' nen she'll say,
"Clear out o' my way!
They's time fer work, an' time fer play!
Take yer dough, an' run, child, run!
Er I cain't git no cookin' done!"

When our hired girl 'tends like she's mad,
An' says folks got to walk the chalk
When she's around, er wisht they had!
I play out on our porch an' talk
To Th' Raggedy Man 'at mows our lawn;
An' he says, "Whew!" an' nen leans on
His old crook-scythe, and blinks his eyes,
An' sniffs all 'round an' says, "I swawn!
Ef my old nose don't tell me lies,

It 'pears like I smell custard-pies!"
An' nen he'll say,
"Clear out o' my way!
They's time fer work, an' time fer play!
Take yer dough, an' run, child, run!
Er she cain't git no cookin' done!"

Wunst our hired girl, when she
Got the supper, an' we all et,
An' it wuz night, an' Ma an' me
An' Pa went wher' the "Social" met, —
An' nen when we come home, an' see
A light in the kitchen door, an' we
Heerd a maccordeun, Pa says, "Lan'-
O'-Gracious! who can her beau be?"
An' I marched in, an' 'Lizabuth Ann
Wuz parchin' corn fer The Raggedy Man!
Better say,
"Clear out o' the way!
They's time fer work, an' time fer play!
Take the hint, an' run, child, run!
Er we cain't git no courtin' done!"

07. A Barefoot Boy

A barefoot boy! I mark him at his play —
For May is here once more, and so is he, —
His dusty trousers, rolled half to the knee,
And his bare ankles grimy, too, as they:
Cross-hatchings of the nettle, in array
Of feverish stripes, hint vividly to me
Of woody pathways winding endlessly
Along the creek, where even yesterday

He plunged his shrinking body—gasped and shook —
Yet called the water "warm," with never lack
Of joy. And so, half enviously I look
Upon this graceless barefoot and his track, —
His toe stubbed —ay, his big toe-nail knocked back
Like unto the clasp of an old pocketbook.

08. The Old Swimmin'-Hole

Oh! the old swimmin'-hole! whare the crick so still and deep
Looked like a baby-river that was laying half asleep,
And the gurgle of the worter round the drift jest below
Sounded like the laugh of somcthing we onc't ust to know
Before we could remember anything but the eyes
Of the angels lookin' out as we left Paradise;
But the merry days of youth is beyond our controle,
And it's hard to part ferever with the old swimmin'-hole.

Oh! the old swimmin'-hole! In the happy days of yore,
When I ust to lean above it on the old sickamore,
Oh! it showed me a face in its warm sunny tide
That gazed back at me so gay and glorified,
It made me love myself, as I leaped to cares
My shadder smilin' up at me with sich tenderness.
But them days is past and gone, and old Time's tuck his toll
From the old man come back to the old swimmin'-hole.

Oh! the old swimmin'-hole! In the long, lazy days
When the humdrum of school made so many run-a-ways,
How pleasant was the jurney down the old dusty lane,
Whare the tracks of our bare feet was all printed so plane
You could tell by the dent of the heel and the sole
They was lots o' fun on hands at the old swimmin'-hole.

But the lost joys is past! Let your tears in sorrow roll
Like the rain that ust to dapple up the old swimmin'-hole.

Thare the bullrushes growed, and the cattails so tall,
And the sunshine and shadder fell over it all;
And it mottled the worter with amber and gold
Tel the glad lilies rocked in the ripples that rolled;
And the snake-feeder's four gauzy wings fluttered by
Like the ghost of a daisy dropped out of the sky,
Or a wownded apple-blossom in the breeze's controle
As it cut acrost some orchurd to'rds the old swimmin'-hole.

Oh! the old swimmin'-hole! When I last saw the place,
The scenes was all changed, like the change in my face;
The bridge of the railroad now crosses the spot
Whare the old divin'-log lays sunk and fergot.
And I stray down the banks whare the trees ust to be —
But never again will theyr shade shelter me!
And I wish in my sorrow I could strip to the soul,
And dive off in my grave like the old swimmin'-hole.

09. There Was a Cherry-Tree

There was a cherry-tree. Its bloomy snows
Cool even now the fevered sight that knows
No more its airy visions of pure joy —
    As when you were a boy.

There was a cherry-tree. The Bluejay sat
His blue against its white —O blue as jet
He seemed there then! —But now —Whoever knew
    He was so pale a blue!

There was a cherry-tree —our child-eyes saw
The miracle —Its pure white snows did thaw
Into a crimson fruitage, far too sweet
    But for a boy to eat.

There was a cherry-tree, give thanks and joy! —
There was a bloom of snow —There was a boy —
There was a bluejay of the realest blue —
    And fruit for both of you.

10. The First Bluebird

Jest rain and snow! and rain again!
    And dribble! drip! and blow!
Then snow! and thaw! and slush! and then
    Some more rain and snow!

This morning I was 'most afeard
    To wake up when, I jing!
I seen the sun shine out and heerd
    The first bluebird of Spring!

Mother she'd raised the winder some;
And in acrost the orchurd come,
    Soft as a angel's wing,
A breezy, treesy, beesy hum,
    Too sweet fer anything!

The winter's shroud was rent a-part
    The sun bust forth in glee,
And when that bluebird sung, my hart
    Hopped out o' bed with me!

11. The Pixy People

Galingale is a plant of the ginger family.

It was just a very
    Merry fairy dream!
All the woods were airy
    With the gloom and gleam;
Crickets in the clover
    Clattered clear and strong,
And the bees droned over
    Their old honey-song.

In the mossy passes,
    Saucy grasshoppers
Leapt about the grasses
    And the thistle-burrs;
And the whispered chuckle
    Of the katydid
Shook the honeysuckle
    Blossoms where he hid.

Through the breezy mazes
    Of the lazy June,
Drowsy with the hazes
    Of the dreamy noon,
Little Pixy-people
    Winged above the walk,
Pouring from the steeple
    Of a mullein-stalk.

One —a gallant fellow
    Evidently King,
Wore a plume of yellow

In a jewelled ring
On a pansy bonnet,
   Gold and white and blue,
With the dew still on it,
   And the fragrance, too.

One —a dainty lady,
   Evidently Queen
Wore a gown of shady
   Moonshine and green,
With a lace of gleaming
   Starlight that sent
All the dewdrops dreaming
   Everywhere she went.

One wore a waistcoat
   Of roseleaves, out and in,
And one wore a faced-coat
   Of tiger-lily-skin;
And one wore a neat coat
   Of palest galingale;
And one a tiny street-coat,
   And one a swallow-tail.

And Ho! sang the King of them,
   And Hey! sang the Queen;
And round and round the ring of them
   Went dancing o'er the green;
And Hey! sang the Queen of them,
   And Ho! sang the King
And all that I had seen of them
   —Wasn't anything!

It was just a very
    Merry fairy dream!
All the woods were airy
    With the gloom and gleam;
Crickets in the clover
    Clattered clear and strong,
And the bees droned over
Their old honey-song!

12. On Any Ordenary Man in a High State of Laughture and Delight

As it's give' me to percieve,
I most certin'y believe
When a man's jest glad plum through,
God's pleased with him, same as you.

13. Pansies

Pansies! Pansies! How I love you, pansies!
    Jaunty-faced, laughing-lipped and dewy-eyed with glee;
Would my song might blossom out in little five-leaved stanzas

As delicate in fancies
As your beauty is to me!

But my eyes shall smile on you, and my hands enfold you,
    Pet, caress, and lift you to the lips that love you so,
That, shut ever in the years that may mildew or mold you,
    My fancy shall behold you
        Fair as in the long ago.

14. The Prayer Perfect

Dear Lord! kind Lord!
    Gracious Lord! I pray
Thou wilt look on all I love,
    Tenderly to-day!
Weed their hearts of weariness;
    Scatter every care
Down a wake of angel-wings
    Winnowing the air.

Bring unto the sorrowing
    All release from pain;
Let the lips of laughter
    Overflow again;
And with all the needy
    O divide, I pray,
This vast treasure of content
    That is mine to-day!

15. When Early March Seems Middle May

When country roads begin to thaw
    In mottled spots of damp and dust,
And fences by the margin draw
    Along the frosty crust
    Their graphic silhouettes, I say,
    The Spring is coming round this way.

When morning-time is bright with sun
    And keen with wind, and both confuse
The dancing, glancing eyes of one
    With tears that ooze and ooze

And nose-tips weep as well as they,
The Spring is coming round this way.

When suddenly some shadow-bird
    Goes wavering beneath the gaze,
And through the hedge the moan is heard
    Of kine that fain would graze
    In grasses new, I smile and say,
    The Spring is coming round this way.

When knotted horse-tails are untied,
    And teamsters whistle here and there,
And clumsy mitts are laid aside,
    And choppers' hands are bare,
    And chips are thick where children play,
    The Spring is coming round this way.

When through the twigs the farmer tramps,
    And troughs are chunked beneath the trees,
And fragrant hints of sugar-camps
    Astray in every breeze,
    And early March seems middle-May,
    The Spring is coming round this way.

When coughs are changed to laughs, and when
    Our frowns melt into smiles of glee,
And all our blood thaws out again
    In streams of ecstasy,
    And poets wreak their roundelay,
    The Spring is coming round this way.

16. The Funniest Thing in the World

The funniest thing in the world, I know,
Is watchin' the monkeys 'at's in the show!
Jumpin' an' runnin' an' racin' roun',
'Way up the top o' the pole; nen down!
First they're here, an' nen they're there,
An' ist a'most any an' ever'where!
Screechin' an' scratchin' wherever they go,
They're the funniest thing in the world, I know!

They're the funniest thing in the world, I think:
Funny to watch'em eat an' drink;
Funny to watch'em a-watchin' us,
An' actin' 'most like grown folks does!
Funny to watch'em p'tend to be
Skeerd at their tail 'at they happen to see;
But the funniest thing in the world they do
Is never to laugh, like me an' you!

17. Naughty Claude

When Little Claude was naughty wunst
    At dinner-time, an' said
He won't say "Thank you" to his Ma,
    She maked him go to bed
An' stay two hours an' not git up,
    So when the clock struck Two,
Nen Claude says,—"Thank you, Mr. Clock,
    I'm much obleeged to you!"

18. An Impetuous Resolve

When little Dickie Swope's a man,
    He's go' to be a Sailor;
An' little Hamey Tincher, he's
    A-go' to be a Tailor:
Bud Mitchell, he's a-go' to be
    A stylish Carriage-Maker;
An' when I grow a grea'-big man,
    I'm go' to be a Baker!

An' Dick'll buy his sailor-suit
    O' Hame; an' Hame'll take it
An' buy as fine a double-rigg
    As ever Bud can make it:
An' nen all three'll drive roun' fer me,
    An' we'll drive off togevver,
A-slingin' pie-crust 'long the road
    Ferever an' ferever!

19. A Sudden Shower

Barefooted boys scud up the street,
    Or skurry under sheltering sheds;
And schoolgirl faces, pale and sweet,
    Gleam from the shawls about their heads.
Doors bang; and mother-voices call
    From alien homes; and rusty gates
Are slammed; and high above it all,
    The thunder grim reverberates.

And then, abrupt,—the rain! the rain!
    The earth lies gasping; and the eyes

Behind the streaming window-pane
    Smile at the trouble of the skies.

The highway smokes; sharp echoes ring;
    The cattle bawl and cowbells clank;
And into town comes galloping
    The farmer's horse, with steaming flank.

The swallow dips beneath the eaves,
    And flirts his plumes and folds his wings;
And under the catawba leaves
    The caterpillar curls and clings.

The bumble-bee is pelted down
    The wet stem of the hollyhock;
And sullenly, in spattered brown,
    The cricket leaps the garden walk.

Within, the baby claps his hands
    And crows with rapture strange and vague;
Without, beneath the rosebush stands
    A dripping rooster on one leg.

20. The Man in the Moon

Said the Raggedy Man, on a hot afternoon:
    "My!
        Sakes!
            What a lot o' mistakes
Some little folks makes on The Man in the Moon!
But people that's b'en to see him like me,
And calls on him frequent and intimutly,
Might drop a few facts that would interest you

James Whitcomb Riley

Clean!
    Through! —
        If you wanted 'em to —
Some actual facts that might interest you!

"O the Man in the Moon has a crick in his back;
    Whee!
        Whimm!
           Ain't you sorry for him?
And a mole on his nose that is purple and black;
And his eyes are so weak that they water and run
If he dares to dream even he looks at the sun —
So he jes' dreams of stars, as the doctors advise —
    My!
        Eyes!
           But isn't he wise —
To jes' dream of stars, as the doctors advise?

"And the Man in the Moon has a boil on his ear —
    Whee!
        Whing!
           What a singular thing!
I know! but these facts are authentic, my dear —
There's a boil on his ear; and a corn on his chin —
He calls it a dimple —but dimples stick in
Yet it might be a dimple turned over, you know!
    Whang!
        Ho!
           Why, certainly so! —
It might be a dimple turned over, you know!

"And the Man in the Moon has a rheumatic knee —
    Gee!

Whizz!
   What a pity that is!
And his toes have worked round where his heels ought to be —
So whenever he wants to go North he goes South,
And comes back with porridge-crumbs all round his mouth,
And he brushes them off with a Japanese fan,
   Whing!
      Whann!
         What a marvelous man!
What a very remarkably marvelous man!

"And the Man in the Moon," sighed The Raggedy Man,
   "Gits!
      So!
         Sullonesome, you know —
Up there by hisse'f sence creation began! —
That when I call on him and then come away,
He grabs me and holds me and begs me to stay —
Till--Well! if it wasn't fer Jimmy-cum-jim,
   Dadd!
      Limb!
         I'd go pardners with him —
Jes' jump my job here and be pardners with him!"

21. Craqueodoom

The Crankadox leaned o'er the edge of the moon
And wistfully gazed on the sea
Where the Gryxabodill madly whistled a tune
To the air of "Ti-fol-de-ding-dee."
The quavering shriek of the Fly-up-the-creek
Was fitfully wafted afar

To the Queen of the Wunks as she powdered her cheek
With the pulverized rays of a star.

The Gool closed his ear on the voice of the Grig,
And his heart it grew heavy as lead
As he marked the Baldekin adjusting his wing
On the opposite side of his head,
And the air it grew chill as the Gryxabodill
Raised his dank, dripping fins to the skies,
And plead with the Plunk for the use of her bill
To pick the tears out of his eyes.

The ghost of the Zhack flitted by in a trance,
And the Squidjum hid under a tub
As he heard the loud hooves of the Hooken advance
With a rub-a-dub —dub-a-dub —dub!
And the Crankadox cried, as he lay down and died,
"My fate there is none to bewail,"
While the Queen of the Wunks drifted over the tide
With a long piece of crape to her tail.

22. Prior to Miss Belle's Appearance

What makes you come HERE fer, Mister,
So much to our house? —SAY?
Come to see our big sister! —
An' Charley he says ' at you kissed her
An' he ketched you, th'uther day! —
Didn' you, Charley? —But we p'omised Belle
An' crossed our heart to never to tell —
'Cause SHE gived us some o' them-er
Chawk'lut-drops 'at you bringed to her!

Charley he's my little b'uther —
An' we has a-mostest fun,
Don't we, Charley? —Our Muther,
Whenever we whips one anuther,
Tries to whip US —an' we RUN —
Don't we, Charley? —An' nen, bime-by,
Nen she gives us cake —an' pie —
Don't she, Charley? —when we come in
An' pomise never to do it ag'in!

HE'S named Charley. —I'm WILLIE —
An' I'm got the purtiest name!
But Uncle Bob HE calls me "Billy" —
Don't he, Charley? —'N' our filly
We named "Billy," the same
Ist like me! An' our Ma said
'At "Bob puts foolishnuss into our head!" —
Didn' she, Charley? —An' SHE don't know
Much about BOYS! —'Cause Bob said so!

Baby's a funniest feller!
Nain't no hair on his head —
IS they, Charley? —It's meller
Wite up there! An' ef Belle er
Us ask wuz WE that way, Ma said, —
"Yes; an' yer PA'S head wuz soft as that,
An' it's that way yet!" —An' Pa grabs his hat
An' says, "Yes, childern, she's right about Pa —
'Cause that's the reason he married yer Ma!"

An' our Ma says 'at "Belle couldn'
Ketch nothin' at all but ist 'BOWS!'" —

An' PA says 'at "you're soft as puddun!" —
An' UNCLE BOB says "you're a good-un —
'Cause he can tell by yer nose!"-
Didn' he, Charley? —An' when Belle'll play
In the poller on th' pianer, some day,
Bob makes up funny songs about you,
Till she gits mad-like he wants her to!

Our sister FANNY she's 'LEVEN
Years old! 'At's mucher 'an _I_ —
Ain't it, Charley? . . . I'm seven! —
But our sister Fanny's in HEAVEN!
Nere's where you go ef you die! —
Don't you, Charley? —Nen you has WINGS —
IST LIKE FANNY! —an' PURTIEST THINGS! —
Don't you, Charley? —An' nen you can FLY —
Ist fly-an' EVER'thing!...I Wisht I'D die!

23. A Dream

I dreamed I was a spider;
A big, fat, hungry spider;
A lusty, rusty spider
With a dozen palsied limbs;
With a dozen limbs that dangled
Where three wretched flies were tangled
And their buzzing wings were strangled
In the middle of their hymns.

And I mocked them like a demon —
A demoniacal demon
Who delights to be a demon

For the sake of sin alone;
And with fondly false embraces
Did I weave my mystic laces
Round their horror-stricken faces
Till I muffled every groan.

And I smiled to see them weeping,
For to see an insect weeping,
Sadly, sorrowfully weeping,
Fattens every spider's mirth;
And to note a fly's heart quaking,
And with anguish ever aching
Till you see it slowly breaking
Is the sweetest thing on earth.

I experienced a pleasure,
Such a highly-flavored pleasure,
Such intoxicating pleasure,
That I drank of it like wine;
And my mortal soul engages
That no spider on the pages
Of the history of ages
Felt a rapture more divine.

I careened around and capered —
Madly, mystically capered —
For three days and nights I capered
Round my web in wild delight;
Till with fierce ambition burning,
And an inward thirst and yearning
I hastened my returning
With a fiendish appetite.

And I found my victims dying,
"Ha!" they whispered, "we are dying!"
Faintly whispered, "we are dying,
And our earthly course is run."
And the scene was so impressing
That I breathed a special blessing,
As I killed them with caressing
And devoured them one by one.

Christina Rossetti (1830-1894)

Biographical Sketch by Wendi Capehart

I was on a vacation at a lake house with one of my daughters and her two young children. It had rained a lot so we had been a bit cooped up. One afternoon as the weather started to clear we took a drive with the windows rolled down. My four-year-old granddaughter breathed in deeply and said, "That smells delicious. I wish I could eat the wind!" Her brother, aged five, rolled his eyes and said, "Well. You can't eat the wind. You can't even see it or touch it, so you can't put it in your mouth and eat it."

My little granddaughter was offended and she argued back, "I can't see it, but I can see the leaves on the trees moving in the wind, and I can feel it on my face, so I know it's there."

Of course, I instantly thought of Christina Rossetti's poem about the wind:

> Who has seen the wind?
> Neither I nor you.
> But when the leaves hang trembling,
> The wind is passing through.
>
> Who has seen the wind?
> Neither you nor I.
> But when the trees bow down their heads,
> The wind is passing by.

There's a reason people say that Christina Rossetti still remembered how the world looked to children even after she was grown. Although she lived in the city of London nearly all her life, she had an eye, and an ear, for the beauty and wonder of seemingly common, everyday things in the world —wind, trees, flowers, birds, and more.

Christina Rossetti was born near Christmas in 1830, the fourth and youngest of four children born to her parents in four years. She had two brothers and one sister. One of her brothers, Dante Gabriel, grew up to become a well-known artist. He used his sister Christina as a model in some of his paintings. Another brother helped edit a literary magazine and helped his younger sister publish her poems.

Christina Rossetti

The Rossetti household where Christina and her siblings grew up was not very conventional. The did not care very much about fitting in with everybody else. Their clothes were often second hand and might be thirty years old. Other families of their class usually had at least a nurserymaid to watch the children. Most middle class children didn't eat their meals with their parents or spend much time with them. In the Rossetti household, the children and their parents spent most of their time together. Mrs. Rossetti homeschooled her daughters, and the children ate with the family instead of being sent to a separate nursery for meals.

Mr. Rossetti was a writer and a teacher from Italy. He had to leave Italy and move to England because his ideas about government and revolution made important members of the Italian government angry with him. They thought he was dangerous. In England he made friends with poets, writers, and people with some radical ideas for the time. He married a half-Italian, half-English woman who could read in three languages. He only spoke Italian with his children, so they were all fluent in Italian as well as English. He was much admired by political rebels and literary people in his own country, so there was a stream of interesting visitors to the house, and people were always asked to stay for dinner, resulting in fascinating conversations. Christina's brother William later described the "sometimes strange and wild" conversations of the various musicians, writers, statesmen and political conspirators or semi-brigands who visited. The children were never asked to leave the room, no matter how strange the conversations.

Christina lived in London with her parents, and, after the death of her father, with her mother for nearly all of her life. She was shy, but because of the rest of her family, she was able to meet many important people in the literary world.

All of the family was very religious, and perhaps her oldest sister and Christina the most so. Christina was very strict with herself. She gave up chess because she felt she was too competitive and enjoyed winning more than was proper for a good Christian, and she would not go to plays because she felt the actors led immoral lives. When an author she liked included some passages in one of his books that were opposed to religion, Christina pasted strips of paper over all the objectionable passages. She never married, although she was proposed to at least twice, because she did not approve of the religious beliefs of her suitors. However her brother William said she was kind and generous with others. She never was heard gossiping about others and she always assumed the best of their intentions.

As a child she did not read as much as her siblings did, although she did love a children's story book of *The Arabian Nights*. As a young woman she had some serious health issues which often left her very much an invalid, and so she spent more time reading. Some of her favourite books were the Bible, the *Confessions* of Augustine, the *Imitation of Christ*, *Pilgrim's Progress*, and the novels of Sir Walter Scott and Dickens. She loved the poetry of Dante, which she could, of course, read in the original Italian.

When she was a young woman, her father's health declined drastically and he became partially blind, and could no longer work at teaching and translating. All of the children, now adults, tried to help with the family finances. Christina also helped to take care her father before he died, for her brother Dante until he died, and then for her mother as well, in spite of her own poor health.

She had both a strong sense of duty and a generous, compassionate spirit, and performed many acts of charity. She was particularly generous in her work with a charity house that helped women who had fallen into lives of crime to recover and find better ways to support themselves. She doubted herself often, but never doubted God. When she died in her sixties, she was praying.

She wrote many religious poems and stories, as well as poems especially for children. After her death, her brother William republished many of her poems and letters to her family with a tribute to her. He said that her beautiful and lovable character shone in her poems and letters, and that her soul was "as pure, duteous, concentrated, loving, and devoted, as ever uttered itself in either prose or verse."

We hope that you enjoy these poems and find pleasure in meeting this loving and devoted soul.

Christina Rossetti

01. Bread and milk for breakfast

Bread and milk for breakfast,
And woolen frocks to wear,
And a crumb for robin redbreast
On the cold days of the year.

02. There's snow on the fields

There's snow on the fields,
And cold in the cottage,
While I sit in the chimney nook
Supping hot pottage.

My clothes are soft and warm,
Fold upon fold,
But I'm so sorry for the poor
Out in the cold.

03. I dug and dug amongst the snow

I dug and dug amongst the snow,
And thought the flowers would never grow;
I dug and dug amongst the sand,
And still no green thing came to hand.

Melt, O snow! the warm winds blow
To thaw the flowers and melt the snow;
But all the winds from every land
Will rear no blossom from the sand.

04. Hear what the mournful linnets say

Hear what the mournful linnets say:
"We built our nest compact and warm,
But cruel boys came round our way
And took our summerhouse by storm.

"They crushed the eggs so neatly laid;
So now we sit with drooping wing,
And watch the ruin they have made,
Too late to build, too sad to sing."

05. Hope is like a harebell

Hope is like a harebell trembling from its birth,
Love is like a rose the joy of all the earth;
Faith is like a lily lifted high and white,
Love is like a lovely rose the world's delight;
Harebells and sweet lilies show a thornless growth,
But the rose with all its thorns excels them both.

06. O wind, why do you never rest

O wind, why do you never rest
Wandering, whistling to and fro,
Bringing rain out of the west,
From the dim north bringing snow?

07. Growing in the vale

Growing in the vale
By the uplands hilly,

Growing straight and frail,
Lady Daffadowndilly.

In a golden crown,
And a scant green gown
While the spring blows chilly,
Lady Daffadown,
Sweet Daffadowndilly.

08. A linnet in a gilded cage

A linnet in a gilded cage, —
A linnet on a bough, —
In frosty winter one might doubt
Which bird is luckier now.

But let the trees burst out in leaf,
And nests be on the bough,
Which linnet is the luckier bird,
Oh who could doubt it now?

09. If all were rain and never sun

If all were rain and never sun,
No bow could span the hill;
If all were sun and never rain,
There'd be no rainbow still.

10. O wind, where have you been

O wind, where have you been,
That you blow so sweet?
Among the violets

Which blossom at your feet.

The honeysuckle waits
For Summer and for heat.
But violets in the chilly Spring
Make the turf so sweet.

11. On the grassy banks

On the grassy banks
Lambkins at their pranks;
Woolly sisters, woolly brothers
Jumping off their feet
While their woolly mothers
Watch by them and bleat.

12. Rushes in a watery place

Rushes in a watery place,
And reeds in a hollow;
A soaring skylark in the sky,
A darting swallow;
And where pale blossom used to hang
Ripe fruit to follow.

13. Heartsease in my garden bed

Heartsease in my garden bed,
With sweetwilliam white and red,
Honeysuckle on my wall: —
Heartsease blossoms in my heart
When sweet William comes to call,

But it withers when we part,
And the honey-trumpets fall.

14. If I were a Queen

If I were a Queen,
What would I do?
I'd make you King,
And I'd wait on you.

If I were a King,
What would I do?
I'd make you Queen,
For I'd marry you.

15. What are heavy?

What are heavy? sea-sand and sorrow:
What are brief? to-day and to-morrow:
What are frail? Spring blossoms and youth:
What are deep? the ocean and truth.

16. Stroke a flint

Stroke a flint, and there is nothing to admire:
Strike a flint, and forthwith flash out sparks of fire.

17. There is but one May in the year

There is but one May in the year,
And sometimes May is wet and cold;
There is but one May in the year
Before the year grows old.

Yet though it be the chilliest May,
With least of sun and most of showers,
Its wind and dew, its night and day,
Bring up the flowers.

18. The summer nights are short

The summer nights are short
Where northern days are long:
For hours and hours lark after lark
Trills out his song.

The summer days are short
Where southern nights are long:
Yet short the night when nightingales
Trill out their song.

19. Twist me a crown of wind-flowers

Wind-flowers are anemones.

Twist me a crown of wind-flowers;
That I may fly away
To hear the singers at their song,
And players at their play.

Put on your crown of wind-flowers:
But whither would you go?
Beyond the surging of the sea
And the storms that blow.

Alas! your crown of wind-flowers
Can never make you fly:
I twist them in a crown to-day,
And to-night they die.

20. Brown and furry

Brown and furry
Caterpillar in a hurry,
Take your walk
To the shady leaf, or stalk,
Or what not,
Which may be the chosen spot.
No toad spy you,
Hovering bird of prey pass by you;
Spin and die,
To live again a butterfly.

21. A pocket handkerchief to hem

A pocket handkerchief to hem —
Oh dear, oh dear, oh dear!
How many stitches it will take
Before it's done, I fear.

Yet set a stitch and then a stitch,
And stitch and stitch away,
Till stitch by stitch the hem is done —
And after work is play!

22. If a pig wore a wig

If a pig wore a wig,
What could we say?
Treat him as a gentleman,
And say "Good day."

If his tail chanced to fail,
What could we do? —
Send him to the tailoress
To get one new.

23. Seldom "can't"

Seldom "can't,"
Seldom "don't";
Never "shan't,"
Never "won't."

24. How many seconds in a minute?

How many seconds in a minute?
Sixty, and no more in it.

How many minutes in an hour?
Sixty for sun and shower.

How many hours in a day?
Twenty-four for work and play.

How many days in a week?
Seven both to hear and speak.

How many weeks in a month?
Four, as the swift moon runn'th.

How many months in a year?
Twelve the almanack makes clear.

How many years in an age?
One hundred says the sage.

How many ages in time?
No one knows the rhyme.

25. What will you give me for my pound?

What will you give me for my pound?
Full twenty shillings round.
What will you give me for my shilling?
Twelve pence to give I'm willing.
What will you give me for my penny?
Four farthings, just so many.

26. January cold desolate

January cold desolate;
February all dripping wet;
March wind ranges;
April changes;
Birds sing in tune
To flowers of May,
And sunny June
Brings longest day;
In scorched July

The storm-clouds fly
Lightning-torn;
August bears corn,
September fruit;
In rough October
Earth must disrobe her;
Stars fall and shoot
In keen November;
And night is long
And cold is strong
In bleak December.

27. What is pink?

What is pink? a rose is pink
By the fountain's brink.
What is red? a poppy's red
In its barley bed.
What is blue? the sky is blue
Where the clouds float thro'.
What is white? a swan is white
Sailing in the light.
What is yellow? pears are yellow,
Rich and ripe and mellow.
What is green? the grass is green,
With small flowers between.
What is violet? clouds are violet
In the summer twilight.
What is orange? why, an orange,
Just an orange!

28. Mother shake the cherry-tree

Mother shake the cherry-tree,
Susan catch a cherry;
Oh how funny that will be,
Let's be merry!

One for brother, one for sister,
Two for mother more,
Six for father, hot and tired,
Knocking at the door.

29. A pin has a head

A pin has a head, but has no hair;
A clock has a face, but no mouth there;
Needles have eyes, but they cannot see;
A fly has a trunk without lock or key;
A timepiece may lose, but cannot win;
A corn-field dimples without a chin;
A hill has no leg, but has a foot;
A wine-glass a stem, but not a root;
A watch has hands, but no thumb or finger;
A boot has a tongue, but is no singer;
Rivers run, though they have no feet;
A saw has teeth, but it does not eat;
Ash-trees have keys, yet never a lock;
And baby crows, without being a cock.

30. Hopping frog

Hopping frog, hop here and be seen,
I'll not pelt you with stick or stone:

Your cap is laced and your coat is green;
Good bye, we'll let each other alone.

Plodding toad, plod here and be looked at,
You the finger of scorn is crooked at:
But though you're lumpish, you're harmless too;
You won't hurt me, and I won't hurt you.

31. The city mouse

The city mouse lives in a house; —
The garden mouse lives in a bower,
He's friendly with the frogs and toads,
And sees the pretty plants in flower.

The city mouse eats bread and cheese; —
The garden mouse eats what he can;
We will not grudge him seeds and stalks,
Poor little timid furry man.

32. A motherless soft lambkin

A motherless soft lambkin
Along upon a hill;
No mother's fleece to shelter him
And wrap him from the cold: —
I'll run to him and comfort him,
I'll fetch him, that I will;
I'll care for him and feed him
Until he's strong and bold.

33. When fishes set umbrellas up

When fishes set umbrellas up
If the rain-drops run,
Lizards will want their parasols
To shade them from the sun.

34. The peacock has a score of eyes

The peacock has a score of eyes,
With which he cannot see;
The cod-fish has a silent sound,
However that may be;

No dandelions tell the time,
Although they turn to clocks;
Cat's-cradle does not hold the cat,
Nor foxglove fit the fox.

35. Pussy has a whiskered face

Pussy has a whiskered face,
Kitty has such pretty ways;
Doggie scampers when I call,
And has a heart to love us all.

36. In the meadow

In the meadow —what in the meadow?
Bluebells, buttercups, meadowsweet,
And fairy rings for the children's feet
In the meadow.

In the garden —what in the garden?
Jacob's-ladder and Solomon's-seal,
And Love-lies-bleeding beside All-heal
In the garden.

37. A frisky lamb

A frisky lamb
And a frisky child
Playing their pranks
In a cowslip meadow:
The sky all blue
And the air all mild
And the fields all sun
And the lanes half shadow.

38. Fly away, fly away over the sea

Fly away, fly away over the sea,
Sun-loving swallow, for summer is done;
Come again, come again, come back to me,
Bringing the summer and bringing the sun.

39. When the cows come home

When the cows come home the milk is coming,
Honey's made while the bees are humming;
Duck and drake on the rushy lake,
And the deer live safe in the breezy brake;
And timid, funny, brisk little bunny,
Winks his nose and sits all sunny.

40. "Ferry me across the water"

"Ferry me across the water,
Do, boatman, do."
"If you've a penny in your purse
I'll ferry you."

"I have a penny in my purse,
And my eyes are blue;
So ferry me across the water,
Do, boatman, do."

"Step into my ferry-boat,
Be they black or blue,
And for the penny in your purse
I'll ferry you."

41. Who has seen the wind?

Who has seen the wind?
Neither I nor you:
But when the leaves hang trembling
The wind is passing thro'.

Who has seen the wind?
Neither you nor I:
But when the trees bow down their heads
The wind is passing by.

42. The horses of the sea

The horses of the sea
Rear a foaming crest,
But the horses of the land
Serve us the best.

The horses of the land
Munch corn and clover,
While the foaming sea-horses
Toss and turn over.

43. O sailor, come ashore

O sailor, come ashore,
What have you brought for me?
Red coral, white coral,
Coral from the sea.

I did not dig it from the ground,
Nor pluck it from a tree;
Feeble insects made it
In the stormy sea.

44. A diamond or a coal?

A diamond or a coal?
A diamond, if you please:
Who cares about a clumsy coal
Beneath the summer trees?

A diamond or a coal?
A coal, sir, if you please:

One comes to care about the coal
What time the waters freeze.

45. Boats sail on the rivers

Boats sail on the rivers,
And ships sail on the seas;
But clouds that sail across the sky
Are prettier far than these.

There are bridges on the rivers,
As pretty as you please;
But the bow that bridges heaven,
And overtops the trees,
And builds a road from earth to sky,
Is prettier far than these.

46. The lily has a smooth stalk

The lily has a smooth stalk,
Will never hurt your hand;
But the rose upon her briar
Is lady of the land.

There's sweetness in an apple tree,
And profit in the corn;
But lady of all beauty
Is a rose upon a thorn.

When with moss and honey
She tips her bending briar,
And half unfolds her glowing heart,
She sets the world on fire.

47. Hurt no living thing

Hurt no living thing:
Ladybird, nor butterfly,
Nor moth with dusty wing,
Nor cricket chirping cheerily,
Nor grasshopper so light of leap,
Nor dancing gnat, nor beetle fat,
Nor harmless worms that creep.

48. I caught a little ladybird

I caught a little ladybird
That flies far away;
I caught a little lady wife
That is both staid and gay.

Come back, my scarlet ladybird,
Back from far away;
I weary of my dolly wife,
My wife that cannot play.

She's such a senseless wooden thing
She stares the livelong day;
Her wig of gold is stiff and cold
And cannot change to grey.

49. A house of cards

A house of cards
Is neat and small:
Shake the table,
It must fall.

Find the Court cards
One by one;
Raise it, roof it, —
Now it's done: —
Shake the table!
That's the fun.

50. The rose with such a bonny blush

The rose with such a bonny blush,
What has the rose to blush about?
If it's the sun that makes her flush,
What's in the sun to flush about?

51. The peach tree on the southern wall

The peach tree on the southern wall
Has basked so long beneath the sun,
Her score of peaches great and small
Bloom rosy, every one.

A peach for brothers, one for each,
A peach for you and a peach for me;
But the biggest, rosiest, downiest peach
For Grandmamma with her tea.

52. Is the moon tired?

Is the moon tired? she looks so pale
Within her misty veil:
She scales the sky from east to west,
And takes no rest.

Before the coming of the night
The moon shows papery white;
Before the dawning of the day
She fades away.

53. If stars dropped out of heaven

If stars dropped out of heaven,
And if flowers took their place,
The sky would still look very fair,
And fair earth's face.

Winged angels might fly down to us
To pluck the stars,
Be we could only long for flowers
Beyond the cloudy bars.

54. If the sun could tell us half

If the sun could tell us half
That he hears and sees,
Sometimes he would make us laugh,

Sometimes make us cry:
Think of all the birds that make
Homes among the trees;
Think of cruel boys who take
Birds that cannot fly.

55. What do the stars do

What do the stars do
Up in the sky,
Higher than the wind can blow,
Or the clouds can fly?

Each star in its own glory
Circles, circles still;
As it was lit to shine and set,
And do its Maker's will.

About AmblesideOnline

This book is one in a series of six, each volume corresponding to the poetry suggestions for Years 1-6 in the AmblesideOnline curriculum.

AmblesideOnline's free Charlotte Mason homeschool curriculum prepares children for a life of rich relationships with God, humanity, and the natural world. Named for the area surrounding Charlotte Mason's schools in England, the AmblesideOnline curriculum is the product of a continuing effort towards a specific vision: to design a course of study that would provide as close a modern approximation as possible of the curriculum created by Charlotte Mason for her PNEU Schools, within the limitations of the current availability of books and materials that match Mason's high standards.

The Advisory, with the assistance of the Auxiliary, lead this work.

The contents of this poetry series, as well as our entire twelve-year curriculum and many other resources, are also available on our website.

amblesideonline.org

Printed in Great Britain
by Amazon